북한 北韓,

A 21st-century Socialist Country
with Economic Transition

Focuses
Train Stations
As a Catalyst for Future Development

Seonhye Sonny Sin

The University of Texas at Austin
School of Architecture
Master of Science in Urban Design

NORTH KOREA
Democratic People's Republic of Korea

SPECIAL THANKS TO
FAMILIES, FRIENDS, AND FACULTY
AT THE UNIVERSITY OF TEXAS AT AUSTIN
FOR ALL THE SUPPORT AND GUIDANCE

ESPECIALLY TO DEAN ALMY AND BARBARA HOIDN

THANK YOU

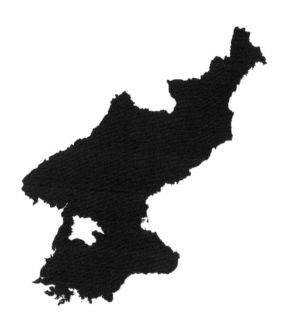

NORTH KOREA
Democratic People's Republic of Korea

Foreword_PATRIA OBSCURA

For much of the world, North Korea is an enigma. What those of us in the west think we know about the country has largely been assimilated through the constructs of political propaganda and myth. The dissemination of information is carefully controlled through the lens of a nationalized media. There is little geographic data on the urban conditions within the country available to outsiders, or its citizens. Even in NASA's well-known composite mapping, Earth's City Lights, North Korea is dark. Undertaking any form of deep analysis is difficult, as information emanating from the country is limited. Viewed from outside, the country stands as dictatorial, militaristic, and exploitative. North Korea is a country whose resources have been appropriated by a hereditary political elite, with scarce provisions remaining for the sustenance of the population at large. The period between the mid-1990s and the mid-2000s, in particular, was marked by severe famine and widespread starvation. North Korea is one of the world's least open economies with strict authoritarian control of the mechanisms of production and distribution. The country suffers from enduring economic difficulties, largely due to extensive spending on its military, which includes the development of advanced weapon systems. This situation has severely constrained the resources needed to adequately sustain the civilian population.[1]

It is within this context that the mappings represented within this publication attempt to illuminate structural and spatial conditions present in the country: the importance of rail transit to trade relationships with China (86.3%) and Russia, the problematic distribution of energy (19 of the 24 million citizens live without electricity), sites of agricultural and industrial production, and settlement patterns, whose morphologies reflect socialist ideology as codified in functionalist planning. This is nevertheless an optimistic project, one that anticipates the potential impact that a change in the governmental policy of improving standards of living may have on the country. In spite of the austerity that has historically characterized the government's centralized approach to the distribution of resources, if this change is to be more than rhetorical, then a new form of economic stimulus is necessary. This study is proposed as an undertaking that projects a social transformation based upon evolution, not revolution, of political agency in the country. It projects a layer of relaxed trade that is based upon the emergence of a newly robust micro-market economy intended to operate as a local informal interchange mechanism. Once activated through programmatic augmentation, the infrastructural opportunities of the rail network are exploited to catalyze new market opportunities that are distributed throughout the country.

The location of resources within the country are identified and documented diagrammatically. These configurations are then strategically assessed, and the information is juxtaposed against the national system of infrastructure to document the potential of the distribution system. These relationships are then reconceptualized at the scale of the entire country. The resultant analysis postulates a new mechanism, "H-City" through which the existing transportation network may be exploited, with the prospect for a modification of how the distribution of production, and the consumption of products, is reorganized across the country. This reconsidered network becomes the generator of new macro and microeconomic potential, exploiting the interface between the rail network, sites of production, and settlement sites. Once activated, a new post-socialist project emerges, one based on the transformative potential of local situations. This system is thereby given a new agency, distributed throughout the country at critical locations. The resultant social and economic benefit occurs beneath the nationally controlled distribution system and opens up the potential for local markets to generate a new capital system based on the interchange of goods and services. This is a form of micro-capitalism that is intended to cultivate the individual initiatives of the population and to immunize it against the program of forced austerity currently enacted by the central government.

The research and documentation presented in this publication is a product of advanced thesis work undertaken in the Graduate Program in Urban Design at The University of Texas at Austin, School of Architecture. The work is positioned as an activist projection of the country, viewed from the south, that through rigorous representational processes, proposes a new framework through which North Korea may reorganize its territory and manage its resources with more sustainable and resilient consequences for its citizens.

[1] The World Factbook, Central Intelligence Agency.

Dean J. Almy III, RA, FFUD

Fellow of the Sinclair Black Chair in the Architecture of Urbanism
Director, Graduate Program in Urban Design

Introduction

North Korea is one of the unique countries around the world. At first, it was developed under socialist ideas. Later, the views combined with totalitarianism. These ideas make the country special, and its isolation from other countries makes it more unprecedented. However, the world's most hidden country has begun to make a different move. Kim Jong-un started a dialogue with the South Korean government in 2016, breaking a decade-long severance between the two countries. Of course, there are both doubtful and positive responses to this change. However, this opens the possibility of a different future of North Korea.

The primary purpose of this book is to make people aware of the potential of the country and see the necessity for further research. North Korea is suffering from lots of urban problems such as food and energy shortages. Still, they have the potential to be a sustainable country with proper national planning strategies. The first step for the future is to research and prepare in advance. However, there is a huge research gap between the years 2007 and 2016 due to political reasons—the research and information on North Korea had barely been updated during this period. Even South Korea was shocked when a documentary in 2015 showed Pyongyang full of high-rise buildings, which is not typical for the city people used to know. This can be another starting point to prepare for a possible future.

This book is not assuming Korean unification but only economic transition, which has already begun in North Korea. By looking into socialist countries that transitioned into post-socialist countries, this book points out the ideal economic transition scenario and focuses on how to make this country sustainable.

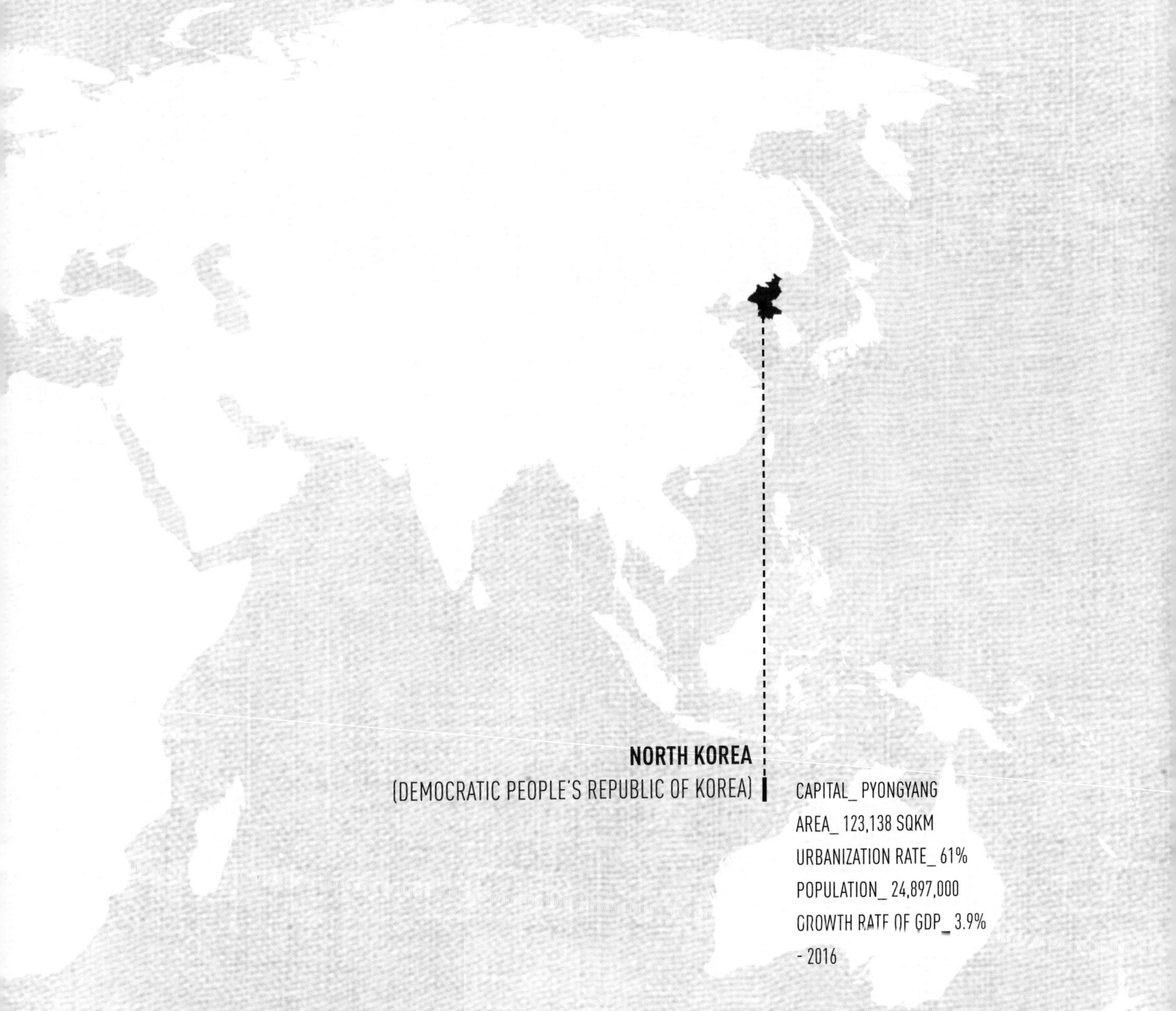

NORTH KOREA

(DEMOCRATIC PEOPLE'S REPUBLIC OF KOREA)

CAPITAL_ PYONGYANG

AREA_ 123,138 SQKM

URBANIZATION RATE_ 61%

POPULATION_ 24,897,000

GROWTH RATE OF GDP_ 3.9%

- 2016

INTRODUCTION_COMPARISON OF PYONGYANG TO OTHER EAST-ASIAN CAPITALS

COMPOSITION

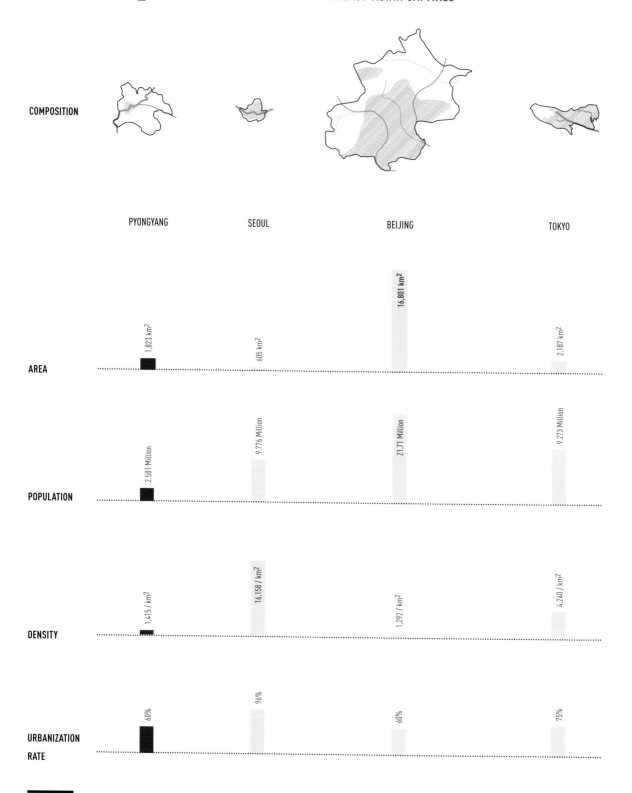

PYONGYANG   SEOUL   BEIJING   TOKYO

AREA

PYONGYANG 1,823 km²
SEOUL 605 km²
BEIJING 16,801 km²
TOKYO 2,187 km²

POPULATION

PYONGYANG 2.581 Million
SEOUL 9.776 Million
BEIJING 21.71 Million
TOKYO 9.273 Million

DENSITY

PYONGYANG 1,415 / km²
SEOUL 16,158 / km²
BEIJING 1,292 / km²
TOKYO 4,240 / km²

URBANIZATION
RATE

PYONGYANG 60%
SEOUL 9.6%
BEIJING 60%
TOKYO 75%

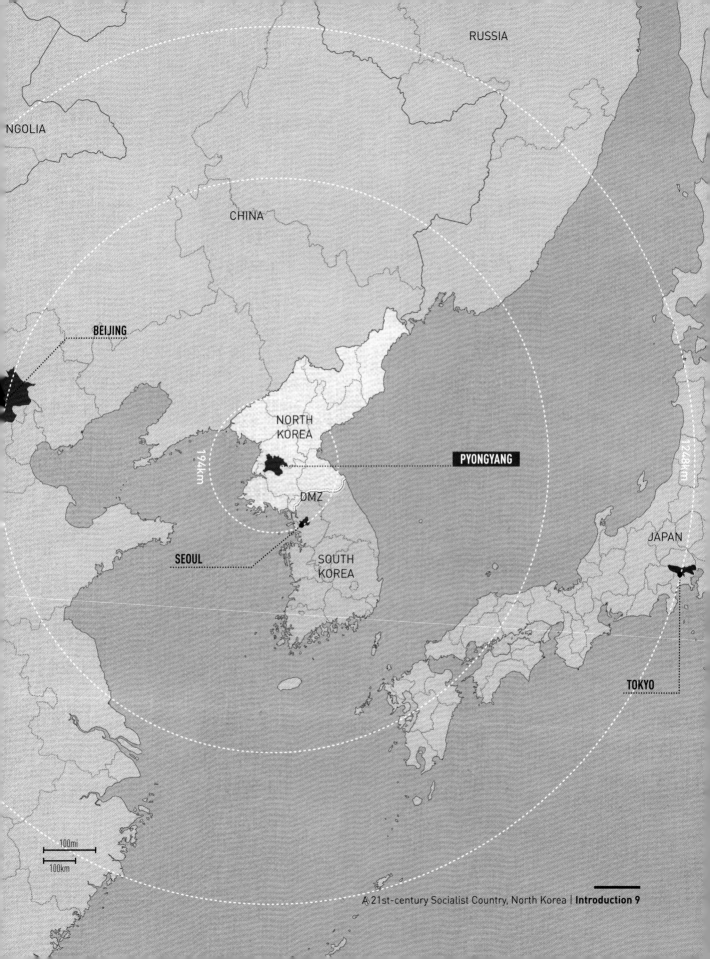

RUSSIA

NGOLIA

CHINA

BEIJING

NORTH
KOREA

PYONGYANG

194km

DMZ

SEOUL

SOUTH
KOREA

JAPAN

1248km

TOKYO

100mi
100km

A 21st-century Socialist Country, North Korea | **Introduction 9**

Socialized
North Korea

1

01

The transition from a socialist city to a post-socialist city causes lots of changes in the economy, politics, and even in the urban structure. North Korea needs to prepare for the future in advance to prevent the typical issues that follow when transitioning to a post-socialist city, such as imprudent development, expansion of a central business district, suburbanization, and residential segregation.

Socialized Countries and Their Transitions

From the start to the transition to a post-socialist country

The definition of "socialist country" is simply a country that was developed under socialist ideals. However, there are no actual cities we can define as a socialist city, only a socialized city as R.A. French asserted. The word socialism was first used in 1827 by Robert Owen and his companies. This concept was established as an opposition to capitalism. At that time, many cities were becoming more significant with technological development. These developments made people gather to cities and thus this concentration of people in one place created lots of urban problems. Therefore, socialists insisted that there be balance in urban and suburban areas. Their main ideas were for balance and equality. Unlike other political or social ideas, socialism tried to solve problems by planning their cities. However, these ideas often failed. Most socialist countries have shifted their plans of action and have become post-socialist countries.

At "post-socialist" country is simply a socialist country that has gone through an economic transition, sometimes happened with political transition too. The transition starts within the non-physical systems and expands into the actual urban structure. The most important part here is, as we can see from past post-socialist cities, they went through several obstacles. Historically, we can divide them into two types according to this process. One is the gradualist approach and the other is the big-bang approach. If North Korea decided to take economic transition, and they didn't prepare, the capital input could be a stimulus to urban development like China, but it may mean they lose the character of a socialist country, as East Berlin did.

Furthermore, this transition for North Korea is already happening. After the death of Kim Il-sung, their first dictator, the food production dropped significantly and 330,000 people died by famine. In order to solve this problem, in 2002 the government established a market economy. Now, there are around 400 official markets in North Korea, as well as uncountable illegal markets referred to as Jangmadangs. As described, this transition is happening already and those markets play the most important role in the current North Korean economy. However, to go through an economic transition, there are more elements to look into.

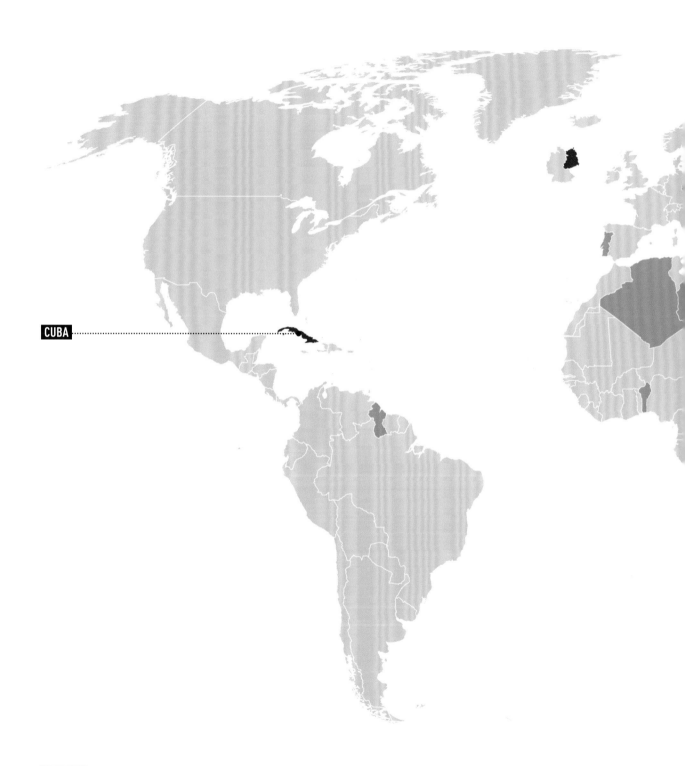

CUBA

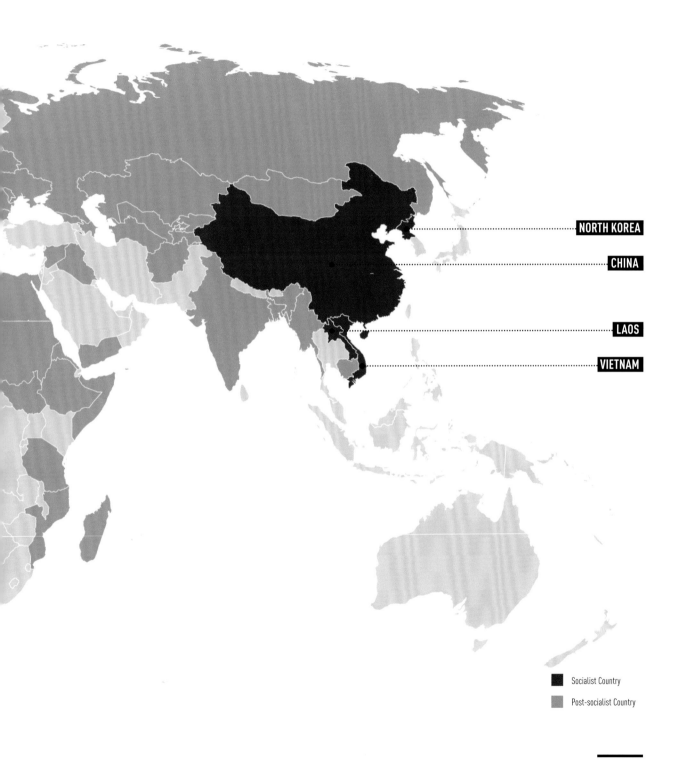

NORTH KOREA

CHINA

LAOS

VIETNAM

Socialist Country

Post-socialist Country

SOCIALIST CONCEPTS_ WITH THE TIMELINE

KARL MARX **FRIEDRICH ENGELS** **ARTURO SORIO Y MATA**

1847
PRINCIPLES OF COMMUNISM

1882
LINEAR CITY

Socialism started as a counter effect of urbanism. As history depicts, the idea had developed within the Soviet Union, until its dissolution in 1990. One interesting fact is that urban planning is part of socialism's main strategy.

In the nineteenth century Karl Marx and Friedrich Engels defined five urban planning strategies. They believed that every urban issue that arose was due to density, so the first strategy was for an anti-metropolitan. The second was for an anti-urban regeneration, which ended up not being helpful in improving urban-housing quality based on their opinions. The third main strategy was to combine city and agricultural land. They thought imprudent developments were another issue that came with high density, so they argued that the city should be developed under plans. And lastly, they believed in centralized control and regulation by a government. According to their ideas, governments should possess all the land and control all production in order to enforce regulations.

Based on those ideas, three foundational theories formed concerning socialist-city planning. The first theory was born from Vladimir Lenin. The second theory was the Linear City concept. And the third theory was the Garden City concept, established by Ebenezer Howard.

Vladimir Lenin put Marx and Engels's principles into practice using six strategies: First, housing should be separated from factories to protect the residential district. Second, the landscape should surround factories to

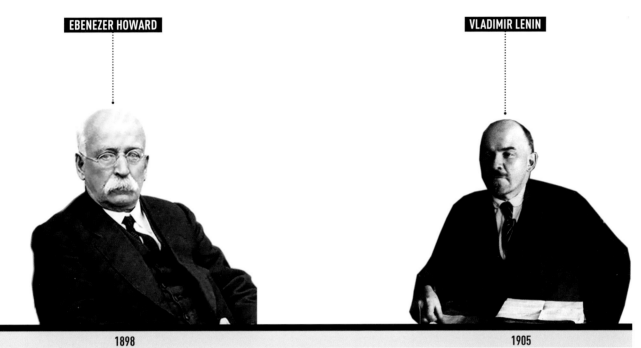

EBENEZER HOWARD	VLADIMIR LENIN
1898	**1905**
GARDEN CITIES OF TOMORROW	MARXISM AND LENINISM

block pollution. Third, to reduce commuting time and energy, all amenities should be placed evenly. Forth, the city center should be an educational space for socialism surrounded by cultural buildings. Fifth, governments should encourage public transportation instead of personal vehicles. Last, a land-use plan should be based on socialist ideology or technical concern.

The Linear City theory was about how a city can be expanded. There have been multiple practitioners who have pushed for a Linear City, including Milutin and Le Corbusier. The main idea there is the same. Along with a major transit corridor, a city is expanded parallel. The purpose is to maintain spatial equality. With the Linear City theory, every house would have a similar distance to transportation, industries, and amenities.

The combination of agriculture in a city was inspired by Ebenezer Howard's Garden City plan. This theory was about finding another way that a city can be expanded. If a city grows over the population of 58,000, it should create satellite cities with only 32,000 people in each. Those cities would then be connected with train tracks and roads. Moreover, each city would be surrounded by a green belt which blocks further expansion.

8 PRINCIPLES OF SOCIALIST DEVELOPMENT_IN NORTH KOREA

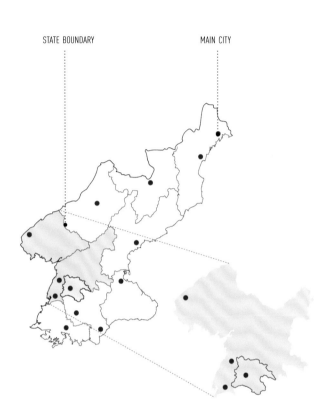

STATE BOUNDARY   MAIN CITY

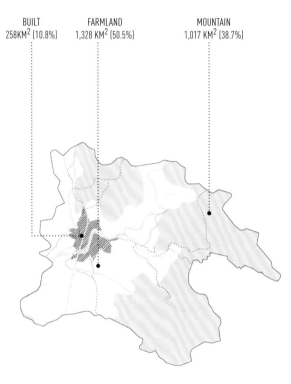

BUILT
258KM^2 (10.8%)

FARMLAND
1,328 KM^2 (50.5%)

MOUNTAIN
1,017 KM^2 (38.7%)

NATIONAL / STATE SCALE

CITY SCALE: PYONGYANG

01 BALANCED DEVELOPMENT

Every states in North Korea have at least one main city and the government has tried to distribute them evenly otherwise unbalanced developments occur and bring about an unequal social structure.

02 SELF-SUSTAINED STATE

Each state was planned to be self-sustaining. Not only is it part of the socialist-planning strategy but is also meant to prepare for wartime, so that if one state gets attacked, others can survive.

03 LIMITED CITY GROWTH

To avoid metropolitans, controlling city size is essential. Socialists suggest surrounding a city with a vast landscape to limit city growth.

04 LANDSCAPE IN THE CITY

Landscape in the socialist city has an important role, not only on the outskirts but inside of the city. The green area is to prevent urban problems that occur from density and provides space to breathe and rest.

RESIDENTIAL AREA INDUSTRIAL AREA POLITICAL CENTER GREEN SPACE MILITARY FACILITY   RESIDENTIAL BUILDING GARDEN COMMUNITY CENTER NEIGHBORHOOD CENTER

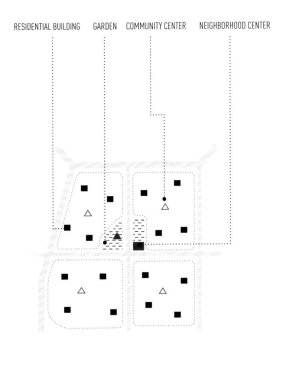

CITY CENTER SCALE: PYONGYANG

NEIGHBORHOOD SCALE: MICRO-DISTRICT

05 STRICT LAND-USE PLAN

The land-use plan of Pyongyang was set in the 1950s and has continued. Based on their regulations, one building should have only one program, and the zoning plan decides it.

06 THE FUNCTION OF CENTER

In most city centers, there is a Central Business District with the highest density. However, in a socialist city, the central area is for educational and public purposes with lower density levels, such as a museum or library.

07 EQUAL DISTRIBUTION

Every socialist strategy is related to equality. It is applied to the neighborhood scale as well. Every program is distributed evenly following the neighborhood unit concept called a micro-district.

08 LIMITED JOURNEY TO WORK

Socialist practicioners insist that the workplace should be within walking distance. By using the micro-district concept, they put a garden, workspace, and retails together.

SOCIALIST CONCEPTS TIMELINE AND THE CHRACTERISTICS_IN NORTH KOREA

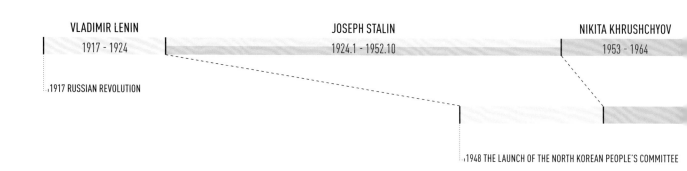

VLADIMIR LENIN	JOSEPH STALIN	NIKITA KHRUSHCHYOV
1917 - 1924	1924.1 - 1952.10	1953 - 1964

1917 RUSSIAN REVOLUTION

1948 THE LAUNCH OF THE NORTH KOREAN PEOPLE'S COMMITTEE

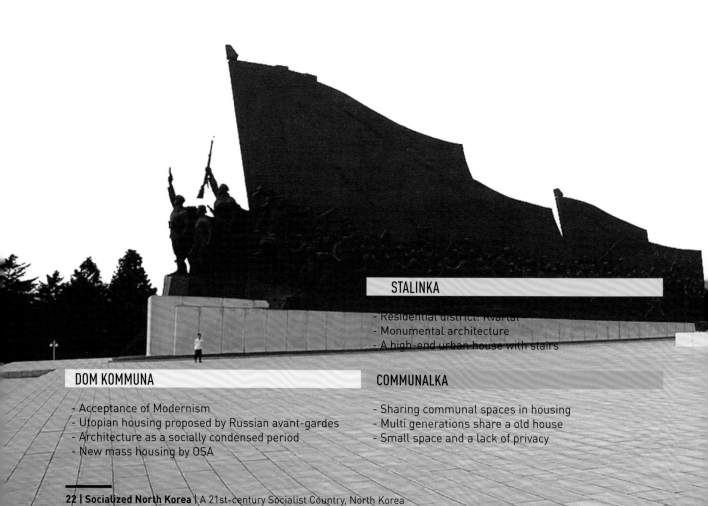

STALINKA

- Residential district: Kvartal
- Monumental architecture
- A high-end urban house with stairs

DOM KOMMUNA

- Acceptance of Modernism
- Utopian housing proposed by Russian avant-gardes
- Architecture as a socially condensed period
- New mass housing by OSA

COMMUNALKA

- Sharing communal spaces in housing
- Multi generations share a old house
- Small space and a lack of privacy

LEONID BREZHNEV
1964 - 1982

1991.12.26 THE COLLAPSE OF SOVIET UNION

KIM IL-SUNG
1957 - 1994

KIM JUNG-IL
1994 - 2011

KIM JUNG-UN
2011 -

1973 NOMINATION KIM JUNG-IL AS THE SUCCESSOR

KHRUSHCHEVKA

- Micro district
- Pre-fab building
- Standardization, Mass production
- Narrow and homogeneous indoor space

POST-KHRUSHCHEVKA

- Aesthetic improvement
- Diversity in housing
- Various pre-fab building

ECONOMIC TRANSITION_THE TYPICAL PROCESS OF ECONOMIC TRANSITION

CURRENT STATE OF
NORTH KOREA

Traditional Socialist Economy ❯ Reformed Socialism Economy ❯ Market Socialism Economy ❯

As a planned and centered economy, it is under the govenment controls

Reformed Socialism Economy is the first step to solve the problem of the inefficient planned economy but still resect market economy but only increase efficiency.

By admitting the limit of a centralized and planned economy, the government makes black markets to an official and coexists of the market and planned economy.

Economic Transition ❯ Influence to Various Area ❯ Impact on Urban Structure

Gradualist Approach
Big Bang Approach

Population
Industry
Energy System
Housing Market
...

Imprudent development
Expansion of Central Business District
Suburbanization
Residential segregation

LIST OF ECONOMIC TRANSITION COUNTRIES (34 countries)

1 Bosnia And Herzegovina
2 Croatia
3 Macedonia
4 Slovenia
5 Montenegro
6 Serbia
7 Estonia
8 Lithuania
9 Latvia
10 Armenia
11 Azerbaijan
12 Belarus

13 Georgia
14 Kazakhstan
15 Kyrgyz Republic
16 Moldova
17 Russian Federation
18 Tajikistan
19 Turkmenistan
20 Ukraine
21 Uzbekistan
22 Czech Republic
23 Slovak Republic
24 Albania

25 Bulgaria
26 Hungary
27 Poland
28 Romania

29 China
30 Cambodia
31 Laos
32 Myanmar
33 Mongolia
34 Vietnam

Transition Countries in Asia

_GRADUALIST AND BIG BANG APPROACHES

Gradualist Approach   Big Bang Approach

HUNGARY
(FOR 40 YEARS)

CZECH REPUBLIC
(FOR 41 YEARS)

POLAND
(FOR 44 YEARS)

CHINA
(FOR 70 YEARS)

LAOS
(FOR 44 YEARS)

CUBA
(FOR 61 YEARS)

EAST GERMANY
(FOR 41 YEARS)

VIETNAM
(FOR 74 YEARS)

CAMBODIA
(FOR 16 YEARS)

There are two types of economic transition. One is called a big-bang approach, which means an unexpected shift, for example: the countries after the collapse of the Soviet Union. Because those countries did not have time to prepare for this sudden change, the impact affected all areas such as population, industry, energy systems, and the housing market, even the urban structure of these countries. On the other hand, a gradualist approach is usually relevant to transitioning countries in Asia. They become a socialist country late or last longer than countries with big bang approach. That means they had more time to prepare for their economic transition. That way, they were able to shift their systems gradually.

CHANGES IN 10 YEAR AFTER THE TRANSITION

1,217,000 People
Moved From East Berlin to West Berlin

5 % Increase
The Number of Housing in East Berlin

RESIDENTIAL SEGREGATION

as a following result of
suburbanization

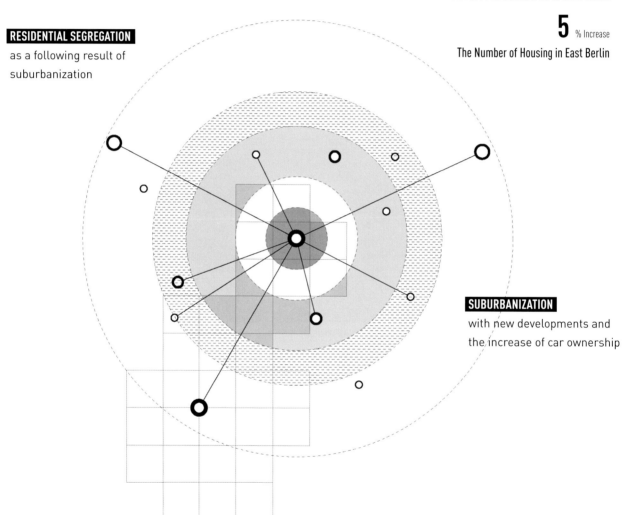

SUBURBANIZATION

with new developments and
the increase of car ownership

IMPRUDENT DEVELOPMENT

with uncontrolled investments
especially foreign capital

EXPANSION OF CBD

replacing the political center of
socialist cities such as museum and
library

SOCIALIST CITY

MONUMENTAL AND EDUCATIONAL PURPOSE

CAPITALIST CITY

CENTRAL BUSINESS DISTRICT

Economic transition does not affect the economy only, it largely affects urban structures. There are four main changes that past post-socialist countries have suffered.

01 IMPRUDENT DEVELOPMENT
When the economic transition occurs, lots of investments will come in, especially lots of foreign investments, which bring a positive effect on economic growth. This sudden input is accompanied by imprudent development. This uncontrolled development can ruin the existing urban structure and character.

02 SUBURBANIZATION
Investors are looking for more comfortable land to develop. In that case, the area within the city is not ideal, where it's already fully developed. Therefore, they look at other areas like the outskirts of the city. New stores and housing is built in those areas, and people start to move farther out. This tendency causes suburbanization, which leads to inner-city decline.

03 RESIDENTIAL SEGREGATION
Residential segregation is the following result of suburbanization. After an economic transition, people start to get their own cars and commute long distances. Moreover, since people start moving to bigger cities, the problem of lack of housing becomes worse. As a result, lots of cheap housing is built in the suburbs, further causing residential segregation.

04 EXPANSION OF CENTRAL BUSINESS DISTRICT
The center of a socialist city is for political education and the public, and would include huge squares. Therefore, this area is another attractive area for developers. If economic transition happens without proper preparation, these areas would be new central business districts and expand even further. The public buildings like museums and libraries would be overtaken by businesses and lose their primary intention.

LEARNING FROM EXISTING POST-SOCIALIST COUNTRIES_THE PROCESS OF TRANSITION

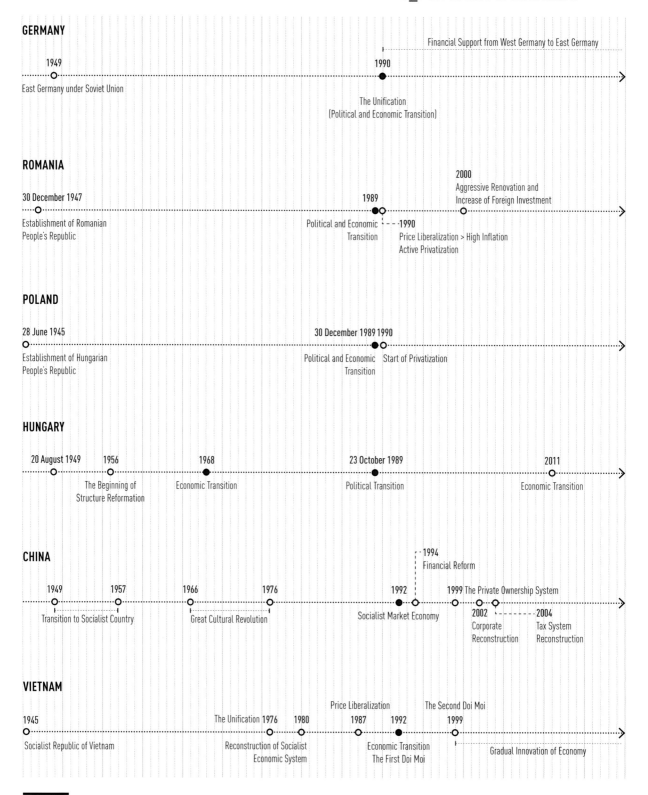

GERMANY

Financial Support from West Germany to East Germany

1949
1990

East Germany under Soviet Union

The Unification
(Political and Economic Transition)

ROMANIA

2000
Aggressive Renovation and
Increase of Foreign Investment

30 December 1947
1989

Establishment of Romanian
People's Republic

Political and Economic
Transition

1990
Price Liberalization > High Inflation
Active Privatization

POLAND

28 June 1945
30 December 1989 1990

Establishment of Hungarian
People's Republic

Political and Economic
Transition

Start of Privatization

HUNGARY

20 August 1949   1956   1968   23 October 1989   2011

The Beginning of
Structure Reformation

Economic Transition

Political Transition

Economic Transition

CHINA

1994
Financial Reform

1949   1957   1966   1976   1992   1999 The Private Ownership System

Transition to Socialist Country

Great Cultural Revolution

Socialist Market Economy

2002
Corporate
Reconstruction

2004
Tax System
Reconstruction

VIETNAM

Price Liberalization   The Second Doi Moi

1945   The Unification 1976   1980   1987   1992   1999

Socialist Republic of Vietnam

Reconstruction of Socialist
Economic System

Economic Transition
The First Doi Moi

Gradual Innovation of Economy

_THE FORM AND THE CHARACTERISTICS OF TRANSITION

	The Form of Transition	Political and Economic Characteristics
Russian (Russia)	Confrontation of Dominating Elites (Conservative and Progressive) ∨ Soviet Dismantlement ∨ Association of Radical Elites and Economic Oligarchy (Collapse of Conservatives)	Etacratism Patrimonial-ism and Capitalism
East European (Romania)	Potential Confrontation of Dominating Elites (Unshaped Progressive Group) ∨ Regional Mass Upheavals, Internal Power Struggle ∨ Preservation of Dominating Elites (Elimination of Specific Faction)	Authoritarianism + Populism Looting Capitalism
Mid-east European (Poland, Hungary)	Political Compromise of Progressive Elites and Anti-elites Groups (Isolation of Conservative Group) ∨ Partial Replacement of Political Elites Preservation of Technical and Business Elites	Formal Democracy + Populism Transnational Capitalism
Chinese (China, Vietnam)	Political Compromise of Conservative and Progressive Elites ∨ Gradual Economic Transition (Maintenance of Political Hard-line) ∨ Internal Unite of Dominating Elites and the Continuation of the Political System	One-party Dictatorship + Corporatism Bureaucratic Capitalism
Cuban (Cuba)	Potential Confrontation of Dominating Elites (Unshaped Progressive Group) ∨ The Anti-reform Tendency of the Leader ∨ Internal Unite of Dominating Elites and the Continuation of the Political System	One-party Dictatorship State Capitalism with Foreign Capital

Source: Choi and Lee (2009), p.18

COMPARISON BASED ON ECONOMIC TYPOLOGY

	Political Transition	Government Intervention	Privatization	Gentrification Speed	Current GDP (2018)	
North Korea (Present)	N	High	-	-	19,000M (Estimated)	
South Korea	N	Low	Low	High	1,720,890M	
Russia	Y (1991)	High	High	-	1,657,553M	Big Bang Approach
Germany	Y (1990)	Mid	High	High	3,996,759M	Big Bang Approach
Hungary	Y (1989)	Low	High	Mid	15,573M	Big Bang Approach
Poland	Y (1989)	High	High	-	585,782M	Big Bang Approach
Czech Republic	Y (1990)	High	Mid	-	244,105M	Big Bang Approach
Romania	Y (1989)	Mid	High	-		
China	N	High	Low	-	13,608,151M	Gradualist Approach
Cambodia	N	-	Low	-	24,571M	Gradualist Approach
Laos	N	Mid	Low	-	18,130M	Gradualist Approach
Vietnam	N	High	Mid	-	244,948M	Gradualist Approach
Cuba	N	High	Low	Low	87,130M	Gradualist Approach

Source: Pedret, A. (2018). *Pyongyang 2050 Spatial Futures.*
Seoul, South Korea: Damdi

The first lesson North Korea can heed from past post-socialist countries is to prepare and apply for the transition step by step. Most previously European socialist countries went through a sudden economic transition and had to deal with the effects later. Their shifts were simultaneous with the political transition. The sudden change made it more difficult for their governments to control the changes and they suffered from significant scale privatizations and fast gentrification. Learning from European transitions, Asian socialist countries approach to the transition differently. Usually, these Asian countries shift without political transition, so they have a more stable government to control the situation. Historically, they have controlled the timing and the size of privatization, giving them space to adjust to the transition gradually, making the impact smaller. The ideal scenario for the North Korean government will be similar to China's

THE INDICATORS OF ECONOMIC GROWTH

Method of Estimating	All Countries		Low-income Countries		Transition Countries	
	Fixation	System GMM	Fixation	System GMM	Fixation	System GMM
Human Capital	+	+			+	
Local Investment	+	+	+	+	+	+
Share of Exports	+		+	+		
Infrastructure	+	+				+
Inflation Rate	-				-	-
Foreign Direct Investment				+	+	+
Condition of the System	+	+	+			
Large Scale Privatization						
Small Scale Privatization						+
Corporate Reconstruction						+
Price Liberalization						
Trade / Foreign Exchange System					+	+
Competition Policy						

+ : Positive - : Negative

Fixation Estimating

System Generalized Method of Moments (System GMM) Estimating

: Two ways to estimate the effect of indicators on the economic

Source: *Determinants of Economic Growth in Transition Economies: Their Implications for North Korea*
Hyung-Gon Jeong, Byung-Yeon Kim, Jae Wan Lee, Ho-Kyung Bang, and Yi Kyung Hong

or Vietnam's transition.

The indicators of economic growth are different based on the economic structure of countries. The table above shows the indexes of all nations, low-income countries, and economically-transitioning countries with two types of estimating the effects: the fixation and system GMM.

This is because North Korea has the characteristics of both a transitioning country and an underdeveloped country. Based on the table, local investment and foreign investment bring positive effects on economic growth, unlike the inflation rate which has negative effects. In the case of transition countries,

the economy grows with small-scale privatization, corporate reconstruction, and trade/foreign exchange system. As a result, the transition should happen, not only changing the economy but the structural rebuilding.

02

The transition in
North Korea is already
happening. To prevent
the same mistakes that
past post-socialist cities
suffered, this is the time in
which North Korea needs
to prepare for the future.

Transition in North Korea

The current state of North Korea and future economic transition scenario

Based on the research found in Hyung-Gon Jeong's article in the Seoul Journal of Economics (2013), "Initial Conditions, Economic Performance, and Reform Prospects in North Korea," the possibility that North Korea can arrive at an unfortunate situation, much like Azerbaijan and Kyrgyzstan, is high without an economic transition. That means the change is required, not elective for this country.

Even though the transition has also already begun in North Korea as of 2002, they have been using the market economy to complement its unstable distribution system. However, the government is worried about the expansion of the market economy. They want to control of this. As a result, they have been repeating the acceptance and suppression of the market economy since then.

Based on past post-socialist countries, the North Korean economic transition should occur through a gradual process, with significant government intervention, small scale privatization, and high foreign investment, infrastructural improvement, and trade/foreign exchange systems. These strategies are for lowering gentrification speed and minimizing the impacts on the urban structures.

This scenario of economic transition in North Korea can be determined in three stages. The first stage would be by starting to open the market and reforming the economic structure. In this stage, the country opens the domestic market in a limited way, approves illegal markets, and diversifies its ownership system. The second stage would be to intensify the rebuilding that happened in the first stage. Finally, the third stage would be the final preparation for economic transition, by expanding the shift to others such as social and political areas. Through those stages, the government can change the socialist economy to market economy gradually.

ECONOMIC TRANSITION IN NORTH KOREA_TRANSITION OF THE ECONOMIC LAW

1948

The Formation of North Korean Government

1990S

After death of Kim Il-sung
Food production dropped significantly
330,000 people died by famine

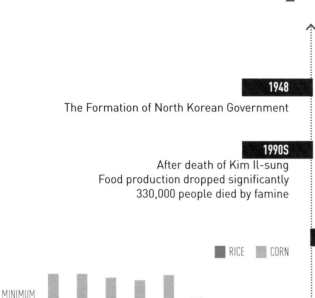

RICE   CORN

MINIMUM
5.3M TON

1989 1990 1991 1992 1993 1994 1995 1996 1997

2002

Partially accepts marketization by law
- Allow companies market activities
- Allow private commercial
- Open public markets in cities

2003

Establish 300 general markets

2007

Suspend market activities to control marketization

> Intensify famine

2012

Extend from some factories and farms to all agriculture, distribution industries

KIM JUNG-UN

Suspend all markets

Connivance
- small commercials on the ground floor of residential building
- Public-private development in housing

PARTICIPATION OF MARKET ECONOMY
_Based on regions

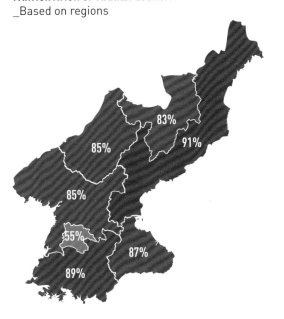

OFFICIAL INCOME AND IN-OFFICIAL INCOME FROM MARKETS
(2013, 133 North Korean defectors)

NORTH KOREAN ARMY
CAPTAIN SALARY = $3

MOST PROFITABLE OCCUPATION (Unit: %)

RETAIL (37.2)

FOREIGN CURRENCY EARNING

CURRENCY USE IN IN-OFFICIAL MARKETS
(Unit: %)

CHINESE

2011   2018   58

NORTH KOREAN

PERCENTAGE OF TRADE EXPERIENCE IN MARKET
(Unit: %)

2011   2012   2013
71.3   69.8   74.4

The North Korean government is based on a socialist economic system that distributes all production equally. However, after the death of Kim Il-sung, their first dictator, they suffered from a severe famine. The government realized that to solve this situation, they need a market economy, so they partially accepted one in 2002. Furthermore, they built 300 public markets throughout the country. However, they wanted to control the markets, so they suspended it again in 2007, which directly intensified famine in North Korea. As a result, they extended the market economy in 2012. The marketization is out of control now.

The government cannot manage it, which means the economic transition is already taking place in North Korea, and it is time for them to prepare for the future that marketization will bring.

MAIN MARKETS OF NORTH KOREA_NUMBER OF MARKETS AND MAIN LOCATIONS

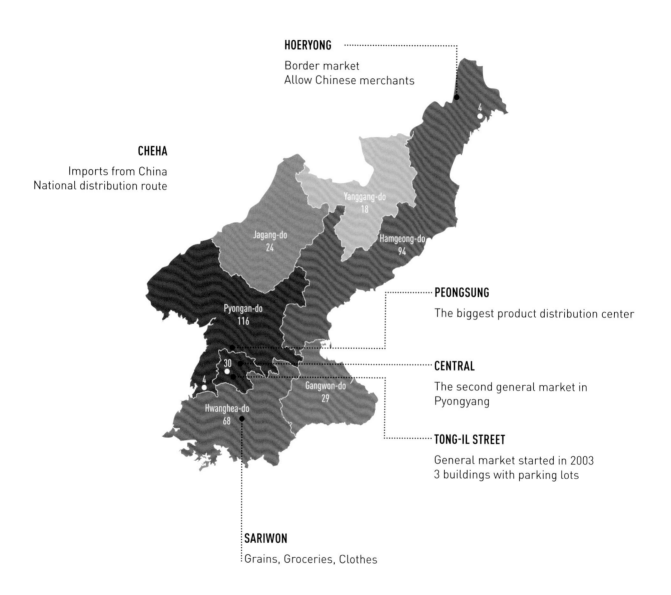

HOERYONG

Border market
Allow Chinese merchants

CHEHA

Imports from China
National distribution route

Yanggang-do
18

Jagang-do
24

Hamgeong-do
94

PEONGSUNG

The biggest product distribution center

Pyongan-do
116

30

4

CENTRAL

The second general market in
Pyongyang

Gangwon-do
29

Hwanghea-do
68

TONG-IL STREET

General market started in 2003
3 buildings with parking lots

SARIWON

Grains, Groceries, Clothes

_TYPOLOGY OF NORTH KOREAN COMMERCE

DEPARTMENT STORE_

There are less than 20 department stores in North Korea for the reason that this kind of retailer is considered to pander to the upper class who want luxury products. These department store buildings usually facilitate shops, storage space, offices, conference rooms, and restaurants.

RETAIL/STREET VENDER_

Street venders have small snacks or drinks. In the past, government was running retails directly but now individuals can occupy with some rents.

GENERAL MARKET_Official Market

This is indoor market which has started in 2003 under the government control. The merchants pay rent to the government and mostly carry groceries and primary products. The closer to the entrance, the rent is more expensive.

JANGMADANG_Illegal Market

This has started naturally in 1990 to maintain a livelihood and held in streets, alleys, or private houses paying a little rent for the owner. It is outnumbered by official markets and getting larger and increases. Usually it starts on outskirts of cities, extends to the riverside or yards inside the city, and becomes part of the city.

SCENARIO OF ECONOMIC TRANSITION_GRADUAL TRANSITION

	Economic Transition	Radical/Gradual Transition	Government Intervention	Privatization	Foreign Investment
North Korea (Future)	Y	Gradual Transition	High	Small Scale	High

STAGE 01   START TO OPEN THE MARKET AND REFORM THE ECONOMIC STRUCTURE

OPEN DOMESTIC MARKET IN A LIMITED WAY

Trade with other countries should be part of the initial plan. It is necessary to encourage foreign direct investment, which brought positive effects on economic growth in past transitioning countries. To start this in a limited way, the North Korean government would determine special economic zones to expose themselves. This process is not only about the geographical location but about all the limitations to minimize the intervention to the local economy. It is reasonable to decide the economic zones based on existing big cities.

APPROVAL OF ILLEGAL MARKET

Approval of illegal markets is the another primary first step. With the illegal markets, all transactions are bound to be unlawful, and this illegal transaction leads to corruption in bureaucratic society, which parasites the markets and seeks private interests. Therefore, it is necessary to expose those markets. Furthermore, those existing markets can be solid foundations for economic transition.

DIVERSIFICATION OF OWNERSHIP SYSTEM

Support for private ownership is the next step in making markets meaningful, strengthened, and activating economic transactions. It can start from the agricultural industry, which is currently a dominant part of the North Korean economy and expand to others like the Chinese model did. The Chinese government determined industries to apply new ownership systems, took time to adjust, based on the result, improved their strategies, and expanded to other areas.

Land Ownership	Infrastructure	Trade / Foreign Exchange System	Gentrification Speed	Impact on Urban Structure
Land Leasing	High	High	Low	Minimum

STAGE 02 INTENSIFY

STAGE 03 FINAL PREPARATION FOR ECONOMIC TRANSITION

INTENSIFY ALL ECONOMIC CHANGES

After the changes in stage 01 get settled, the next step is intensifying all of them, which is expanding the number of industries opened to foreign investment and private ownership systems, and with existing markets, there will be many more new markets. These changes will be catalysts of their declining economy and lives, and the changes will be accelerated through time. At this stage, the government would evaluate their policies, develop, and apply more actively.

STABILIZATION AND EXPANSION

When stage 02 is completed, it is time to prepare for economic transition, which is stabilization. They need to digest all the economic changes and prepare for the completion of economic transition. After that, they can widen the transformation into other parts of the country, such as infrastructure and society.

RECONSTRUCTION OF SOCIAL SYSTEM

In this stage, the government needs to reconstruct its systems aside from the economy. Now that they have a properly working economy, they can look at social networks such as education and health.

DECENTRALIZATION OF POLITICAL POWER

The political climate in North Korea is the most challenging obstacle, although the needs for change are evident. However, they still need to decentralize the political power to a certain level as part of the transition.

New
National Planning,
H-city

2

01

9 Urban Challenges

That North Korea is suffering from

It is hard to say whether North Korea is functioning properly as a country. There are nine urban challenges that make the country dysfunctional. First, North Korea 50% of North Korea is made up of mountains. That means more than half of their land is not easily developed.

Along those mountain lines, there are lots of rivers, however, because most of the precipitation is narrowed to the summer season, they have drought and flooding issues. Therefore, water infrastructure is mandatory in this country, but most of their systems are aged.

Also, the most prominent use of water is hydroelectric, but it's not sufficient enough to serve the entire population because of the deterioration of their facilities.

Lots of other issues, such as insufficient public transportation, come from this shortage of energy. Furthermore, food production is not enough either, mainly, in alpine regions. One interesting fact is that they have enough grain with imports from China, but the balance of nutrition is collapsed.

Even their mobility system does not working correctly. People use the train for long journeys, but in day-to-day life, the bike is the number one mode of transportation in North Korean. They have other options like subways or streetcars, but these often stop running.

North Koreans mostly live in rows of house or detached houses, but only 70-80% of them even have a home, and the stability of these

houses cannot even be guaranteed. Most houses are built at a rapid pace for domestic, and international propaganda use, so these structures are not stable. If considering these facts, the housing shortage problem is more severe than the current working number.

North Korea is currently trading with a minimal amount of countries, and mostly for mineral fuel. Their primary trading system is located along train tracks. The industry here is still based on primary and secondary sectors. Their economy has not gotten better with time. The failure of their economic system is the focal point for all of the challenges. It becomes more apparent when we compare it to South Korea.

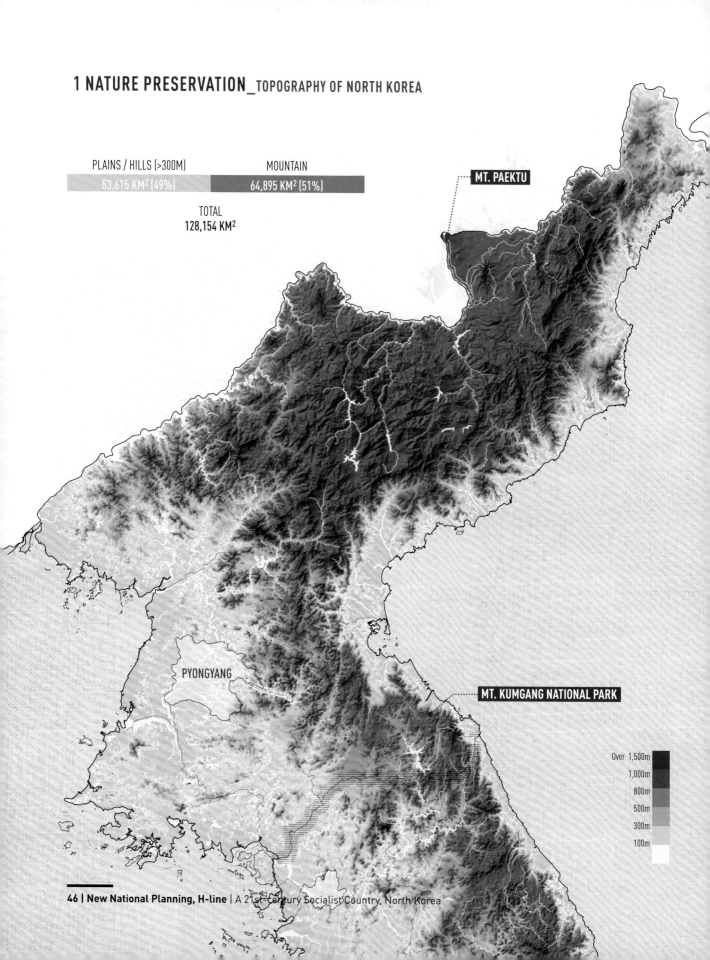

1 NATURE PRESERVATION_TOPOGRAPHY OF NORTH KOREA

PLAINS / HILLS (>300M)	MOUNTAIN
53,615 KM² (49%)	64,895 KM² (51%)

TOTAL
128,154 KM²

MT. PAEKTU

MT. KUMGANG NATIONAL PARK

PYONGYANG

Over 1,500m
1,000m
800m
500m
300m
100m

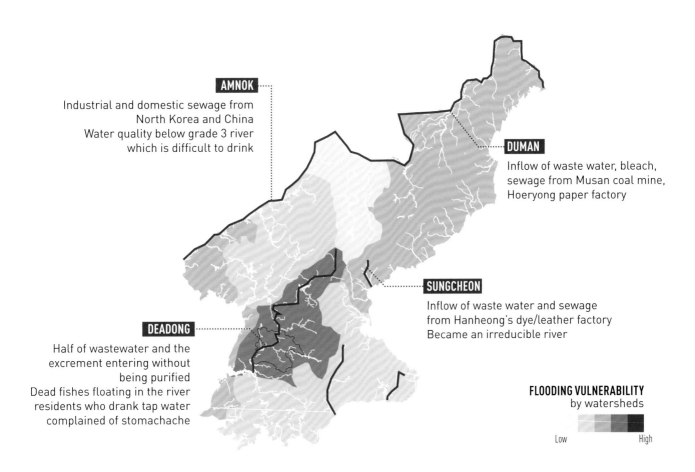

AMNOK

Industrial and domestic sewage from
North Korea and China
Water quality below grade 3 river
which is difficult to drink

DUMAN

Inflow of waste water, bleach,
sewage from Musan coal mine,
Hoeryong paper factory

SUNGCHEON

Inflow of waste water and sewage
from Hanheong's dye/leather factory
Became an irreducible river

DEADONG

Half of wastewater and the
excrement entering without
being purified
Dead fishes floating in the river
residents who drank tap water
complained of stomachache

FLOODING VULNERABILITY
by watersheds

Low   High

PRECIPITATION by month

60% OF ANNUAL PRECIPITATION

Jan Feb Mar Apr May Jun Jul Aug Sep Oct Nov Dec

WATER RESOURCES STRUCTURE and the utilization

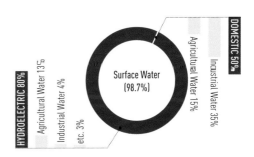

HYDROELECTRIC 80%

Agricultural Water 13%

Industrial Water 4%

etc. 3%

Surface Water
(98.7%)

DOMESTIC 50%

Agricultural Water 15%

Industrial Water 35%

3 ENERGY_THE SUPPLY AND USE

GENERATION CAPACITY by type and location

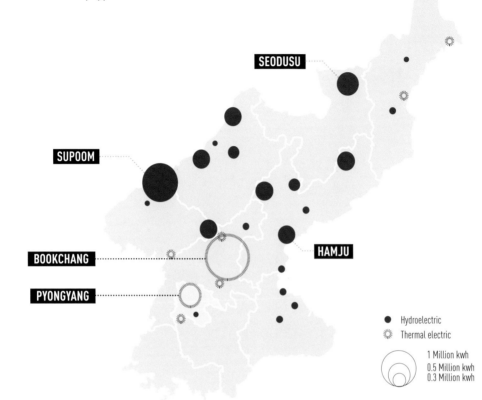

- ● Hydroelectric
- ✳ Thermal electric

1 Million kwh
0.5 Million kwh
0.3 Million kwh

ENERGY SUPPLY WAY by ratio

Distribution 20.6%
Market 44.1%
Self-supply 35.3%

DOMESTIC ENERGY USE by ratio

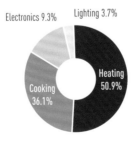

Electronics 9.3% Lighting 3.7%
Heating 50.9%
Cooking 36.1%

ENERGY SOURCE by ratio

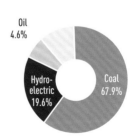

Oil 4.6%
Hydro-electric 19.6%
Coal 67.9%

ENERGY OUTPUT from 1990 to 2014

ELECTRIC ENERGY in billion kwh

Year	Hydroelectric	Thermal electric
1990	Hydroelectric 156	Thermal electric 121
2000	102	92
2005	131	84
2010	134	103
2015	100	90

4 FOOD_THE PRODUCTION AND SHORTAGE

DAILY FOOD SUPPLY by rank

Rank	Supply	Recipient
1	900g	Harmful Occupation
2	800g	Coal Miner
3	700g	General Ocupation
4	600g	College Student, Patient
5	500g	Middle School Student
6	400g	Elementary School Student
7	300g	Eldery, Kindergartener
8	200g	2-4 year olds, Prisoner
9	100g	Younger than 1 years old

FOOD PRODUCTION by month

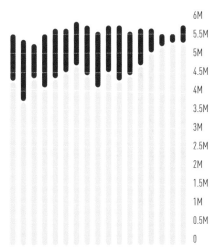

NUTRITION DIFICIENCY LEVEL by regions

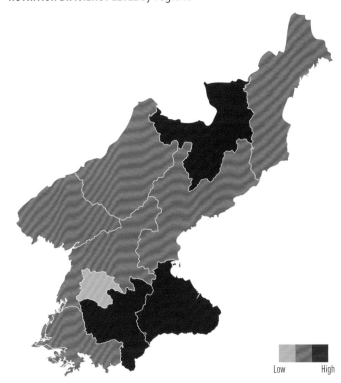

Low   High

SOURCE OF NUTRITION compared to South Korea

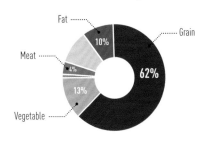

Fat 10%
Meat 4%
Vegetable 13%
Grain 62%

27%
11%
8%
43%

South Korea

The lack of food production in North Korea began in the 1900s. They failed to develop their own agricultural administration, called Juche Nongbub. Because of the collective farming that comes with socialism, production is at a decline. Even in the 1980s, the average amount of production was only 4.15 million tons, which is two million less than the minimum requirement. This made the North Korean government decide to reduce rations from 700g to 546g per person (22% reduction). After 1990, most other socialist countries like the USSR stopped supporting North Korea, and this made their situation worse.

5 MOBILITY_THE TYPOLOGIES

SOUTH KOREA | NORTH KOREA

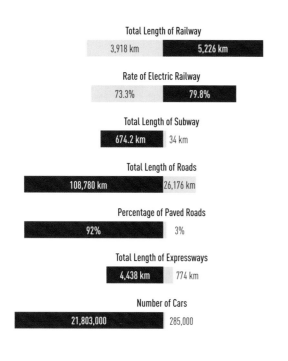

Total Length of Railway
3,918 km   5,226 km

Rate of Electric Railway
73.3%   79.8%

Total Length of Subway
674.2 km   34 km

Total Length of Roads
108,780 km   26,176 km

Percentage of Paved Roads
92%   3%

Total Length of Expressways
4,438 km   774 km

Number of Cars
21,803,000   285,000

TYPOLOGIES OF TRANSPORTATION in North Korea

TRAIN

The most common for long distance journey
International train connected to China and Russia

SUBWAY

Only in Pyongyang, the capital
Utilization by Pyongyang citizen and Tourist

STREET CAR

Only in Pyongyang, Using rails
Using electrical wires in rural area

BUS

Cross-country bus in 6 cities in North Korea
40 routes in Pyongyang

SERVI-CAR

The second common public transportation
Run by military or administry of North Korea

TAXI

Only in Pyongyang, Double-shift system
The fare from $2

CAR

Only the executive members

BIKE

The most common transportation method
No.1 property for North Korean

TOTAL LENGTH OF RAILWAY 1910-2015 in 1,000km

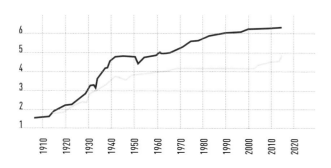

In comparing North Korea to South Korea, there are only two elements worth looking at: the total length of the railway and the rate of an electric railway. Except for those two elements, every other statistic concerning mobility is much lower in North Korea. Because of their energy shortage, most of trains, subways, and streetcars are not operating correctly. Therefore, the most common transportation for a North Korean is a bike. The servi-car is another by-product of governmental dysfunction.

_ROADS AND RAILWAY NETWORK

DMZ

‐ ‐ Main Train Line

—— Local Train Line

—— Road

☐ Main City

6 HOUSING_THE CONSTRUCTION AND SHORTAGE

333-666 people/ha
Population Density

67-135 units/ha
Housing Density

70-80 %
Housing Penetration

1M Housing
New Housing Construction Needed

24,897,000
Population in 2016

5,887,471
Total Number of Household

4.22 people
Average Number of Family Member

2M-3M Housing
Old Housing Need to be Improved

HOUSE TYPOLOGY by ratio

Apartment 21%
Detached House 33%
Row House 44%

NUMBER OF ROOM in a house

2 Rooms 65%

SIZE OF HOUSE in North Korea

50-75m² 73%

HOUSING CONSTRUCTION through time

Time	Project	The number of housing built		
Kim Il-sung	1954 – 1956 Post-war reconstruction plan	771,700	18.6%	
	1957 – 1960 5-year plan			
	1961 – 1969 The first 7-year plan	800,000	19.2%	(37.8%)
	1971 – 1976 6-year plan	886,000	21.3%	(59.1%)
	1978 – 1984 The second 7-year plan	750,000 - 1,050,000	25.3%	(84.4$)
	1987 – 1993 The third 7-year plan	290,000 - 340,000	8.1%	(92.5%)
Kim Jung-il	Unknown	300,000	3.75%	(96.25%)
Kim Jung-un	Unknown	300,000	3.75%	(100%)
Total		3,797,500 – 4,147,500	100%	

7 TRADE TO WORLD_MAIN TRADING CITIES IN NORTH KOREA

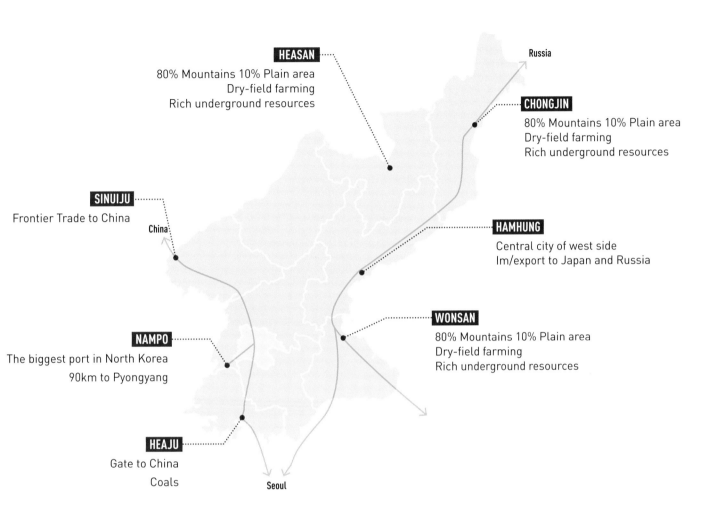

HEASAN
80% Mountains 10% Plain area
Dry-field farming
Rich underground resources

Russia

CHONGJIN
80% Mountains 10% Plain area
Dry-field farming
Rich underground resources

SINUIJU
Frontier Trade to China

China

HAMHUNG
Central city of west side
Im/export to Japan and Russia

NAMPO
The biggest port in North Korea
90km to Pyongyang

WONSAN
80% Mountains 10% Plain area
Dry-field farming
Rich underground resources

HEAJU
Gate to China
Coals

Seoul

THE TOTAL EXPORTS (2008-2017)

THE MAJOR EXPORTS (2015, Billion $)

STEEL

FISH

IRON

CLOTHES

MINERAL FUEL (11.8)

THE MAJOR IMPORTS (2015, Billion $)

PLASTIC GOODS

CAR / PARTS

MACHINERY

ELECTRICAL INSTRUMENT

MINERAL FUEL (7.5)

A 21st-century Socialist Country, North Korea | **New National Planning, H-line 53**

8 INDUSTRIALIZATION_THE STRUCTURE

PERCENTAGE OF INDUSTRIES by States

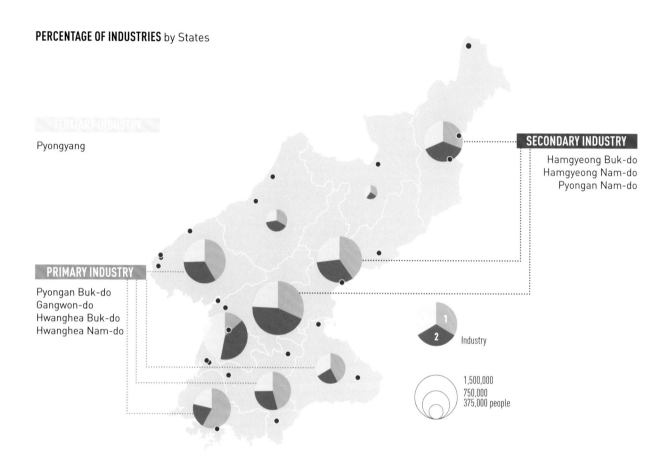

TERTIARY INDUSTRY

Pyongyang

SECONDARY INDUSTRY

Hamgyeong Buk-do
Hamgyeong Nam-do
Pyongan Nam-do

PRIMARY INDUSTRY

Pyongan Buk-do
Gangwon-do
Hwanghea Buk-do
Hwanghea Nam-do

1
2 Industry

1,500,000
750,000
375,000 people

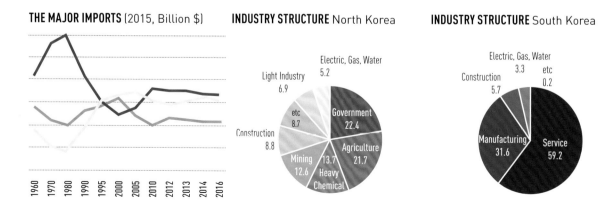

THE MAJOR IMPORTS (2015, Billion $)

1960 1970 1980 1990 1995 2000 2005 2010 2012 2013 2014 2016

INDUSTRY STRUCTURE North Korea

Electric, Gas, Water
5.2
Light Industry
6.9
etc
8.7
Construction
8.8
Government
22.4
Agriculture
21.7
Mining
12.6
Heavy
Chemical
13.7

INDUSTRY STRUCTURE South Korea

Electric, Gas, Water
3.3
etc
0.2
Construction
5.7
Manufacturing
31.6
Service
59.2

9 ECONOMY_MARKETIZATION AND LOCAL ECONOMY

North Korean government is
controling markets and local
economy by limiting physical spaces.

MINE INDUSTRY GROWTH RATE (BY YEAR)

LIGHT INDUSTRY GROWTH RATE (BY YEAR)

GROSS NATIONAL INCOME
(Unit: Billion Dollar)

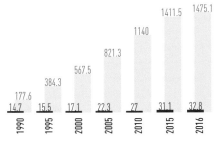

1990	1995	2000	2005	2010	2015	2016
177.6	384.3	567.5	821.3	1140	1411.5	1475.1
14.7	15.5	17.1	22.3	27	31.1	32.8

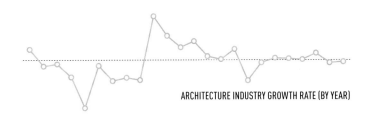

ARCHITECTURE INDUSTRY GROWTH RATE (BY YEAR)

PER CAPITA GROSS INCOME
(Unit: Dollar)

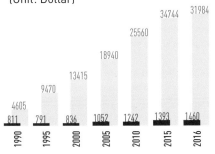

1990	1995	2000	2005	2010	2015	2016
4605	9470	13415	18940	25560	34744	31984
811	791	836	1052	1242	1393	1460

AGRICULTURE/FISHING INDUSTRY GROWTH RATE (BY YEAR)

ECONOMIC GROWTH RATE (Unit: %)

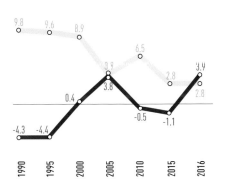

9.8   9.6   8.9   6.5   2.8
9.8   3.8   0.4   -0.5 -1.1 3.9   2.8
-4.3 -4.4

| 1990 | 1995 | 2000 | 2005 | 2010 | 2015 | 2016 |

MANUFACTURING INDUSTRY GROWTH RATE (BY YEAR)

HEAVY INDUSTRY GROWTH RATE (BY YEAR)

SERVICE INDUSTRY GROWTH RATE (BY YEAR)

02

From its beginning,
North Korea has not been
suitable for socialist
planning strategies.
Korea was historically
under one whole system.
Based on the landscape,
each municipality
has uniqueness and
complement each other.

Regional Planning in North Korea

The Failure of Socialist National Planning

The Korean peninsula had been treated as one system historically. Korea is a small country, so it is apparent that it needs different national planning strategies from other big countries. Under the one network, each region had concentrated its characteristics to strengthen it.

However, after the ceasefire agreement between the South and North Korea, each side had been modernized differently. South Korea stuck to the historical strategy, but North Korea did not. This country was developed with socialist planning strategies. One of the main ideas was to make each state self-sustaining, which was not suitable for a small country like North Korea. Because of this strategy, each state did not trade with each other. This planning tears apart the nation into pieces. Therefore, the new national plan for North Korea should be to make the country one system again. The H-city plan uses the train lines to connect the whole country, the foundation for the project. Notably, the main transit corridor shaped like an H has lots of potentials. This line goes from South Korea to China, Russia, and European countries. It can be a significant trade route if North Korea decides to open their country.

The H-line will be a catalyst for future developments, and this development will attract lots of people. This tendency changes the population distribution and urbanization of North Korea. Both of them will be concentrated along the H-line and will form H-city.

To support transit, industries, and developments, a sustainable energy source is crucial. One of the most efficient options is a wind farm, using the characteristics of a country that has lots of mountains. Efficient food production and distribution is another crucial matter in this nation. If the government promotes alpine agriculture along the transit line, they have enough land to feed their population. Finally, they are in need of a new industrial system. This strategy is to prepare for the future in considering existing assets in the country; Keeping primary industries, building stable secondary sectors, and introducing tertiary sectors.

KOREAN PENINSULA_REGIONAL CHARACTERISTICS

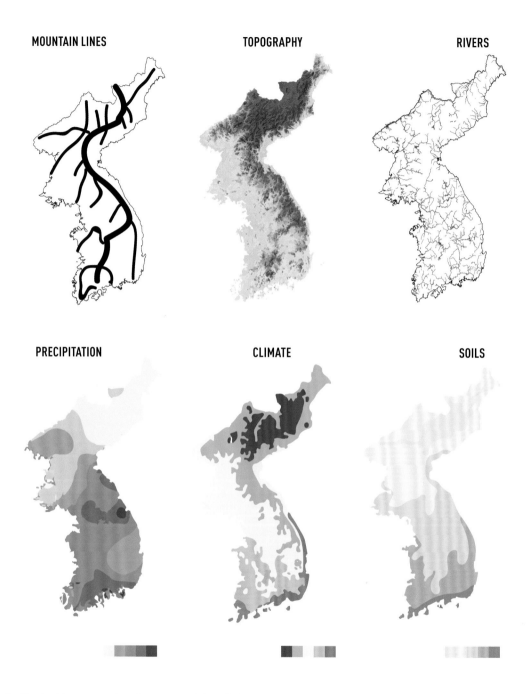

MOUNTAIN LINES

TOPOGRAPHY

RIVERS

PRECIPITATION

CLIMATE

SOILS

Historically, the Korean peninsula works as one mega region. As a smaller country, this strategy was for surviving. Only when each regions work together, can the country work properly, because each municipality has different specialties based on its location and landscape.

_9 MUNICIPALITIES AND ITS CHARACTERISTICS

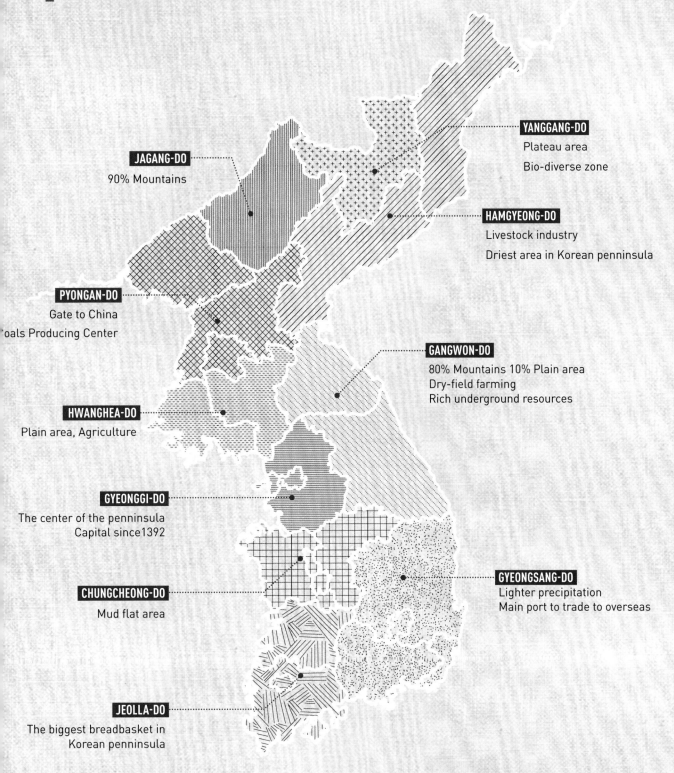

YANGGANG-DO
Plateau area
Bio-diverse zone

JAGANG-DO
90% Mountains

HAMGYEONG-DO
Livestock industry
Driest area in Korean penninsula

PYONGAN-DO
Gate to China
Coals Producing Center

GANGWON-DO
80% Mountains 10% Plain area
Dry-field farming
Rich underground resources

HWANGHEA-DO
Plain area, Agriculture

GYEONGGI-DO
The center of the penninsula
Capital since1392

GYEONGSANG-DO
Lighter precipitation
Main port to trade to overseas

CHUNGCHEONG-DO
Mud flat area

JEOLLA-DO
The biggest breadbasket in
Korean penninsula

EXISTING NATIONAL STRUCTURE_REGIONAL CHARACTERISTICS

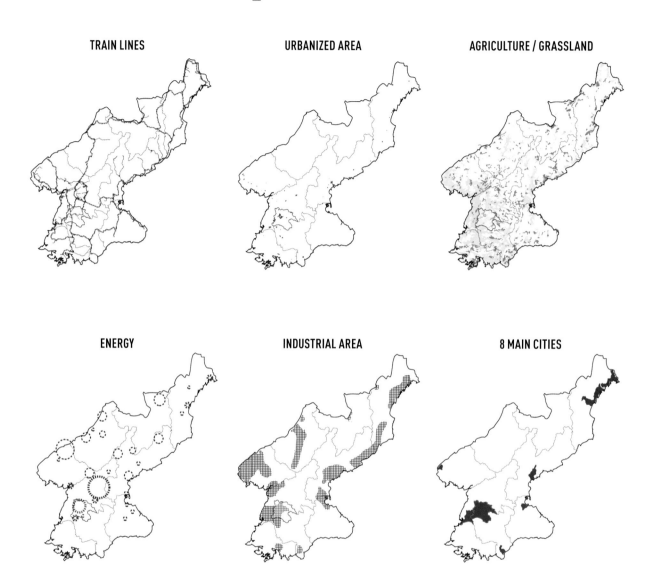

TRAIN LINES

URBANIZED AREA

AGRICULTURE / GRASSLAND

ENERGY

INDUSTRIAL AREA

8 MAIN CITIES

After the separation of North and South Korea, North Korea started to develop their country according to socialist ideas. For instance, each municipality tried to be self-sufficient, they even discouraged trading one another. Most goods were scattered under the guise of even distribution as part of socialist planning but also to prepare for potential wartime—so that if one municipality is attacked, the others would survive. However, these strategies were not suitable for a small country like North Korea. As a result, the country has broken into pieces, and no municipalities have functioned correctly. The failure of national planning is one of the reasons for the unsustainability of this country.

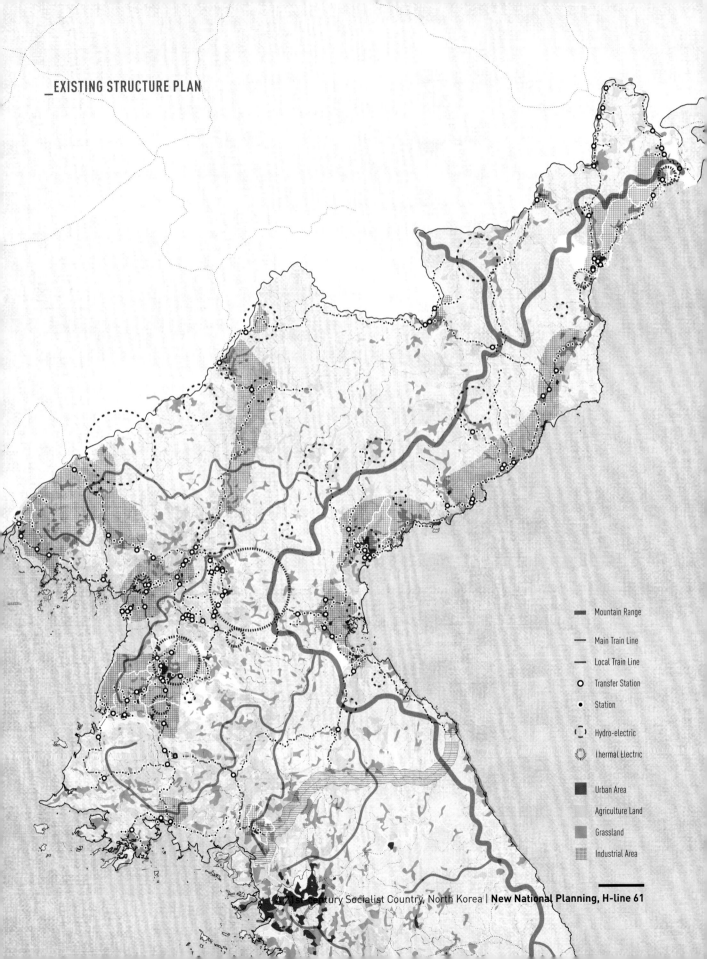

Mountain Range

Main Train Line

Local Train Line

○ Transfer Station

• Station

Hydro-electric

Thermal Electric

Urban Area

Agriculture Land

Grassland

Industrial Area

A 21st Century Socialist Country, North Korea | **New National Planning, H-line 61**

FUTURE DEVELOPMENT SCENARIO_BACK TO ONE WHOLE COUNTRY

   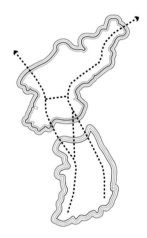

MAKE AS A ONE SYSTEM

FUTURE DEVELOPMENT

-1950

In the past, the Korean peninsula was under one system. It enforced the characteristics of each region to survive as a small country. Each municipality had its role in the country. For instance, the southern side, like Jeolla-do, is the leading rice production area, and the northern side is full of mineral resources.

1950 - PRESENT

After the Armistice Agreement between North and South Korea, the north was developed under socialism, and the south under capitalism. As a result, the north split the country into pieces, but the south did not. This decision has affected their countries more than expected.

FUTURE STAGE 01

The first step toward future development is making national plans to revert North Korea back to one system again. The new national strategies should be based on enhancing current assets such as the four economic hubs in North Korea.

FUTURE STAGE 02

The second stage is stitching the country by transit lines. The h-shape train corridor connects the Korean peninsula to Europe and will be the catalyst for future developments with the four economic hubs. This transportation is the base structure for the new national planning called H-city.

_FOUR ECONOMIC HUBS IN NORTH KOREA

04

03

02

EH 01

Seoul

Tokyo

Shanghai

Economic Hub in North Korea   Flight Route
                                    Water Route
Economic Hub in Other Countries   Train Track

A 21st-century Socialist Country, North Korea | **New National Planning, H-line 63**

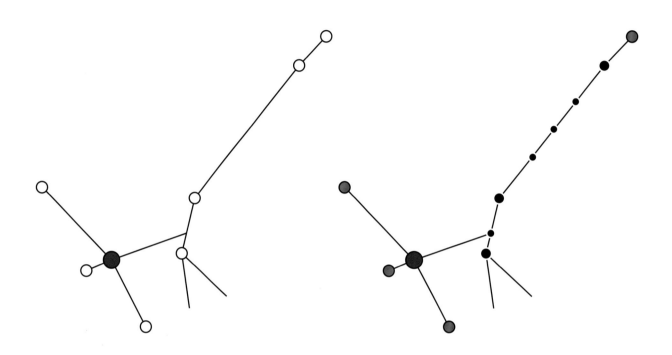

MAIN CITIES WITH H-LINE

INDUSTRIAL SYSTEM

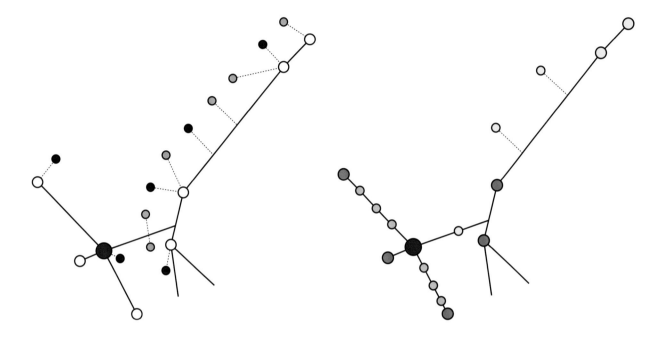

ENERGY SYSTEM

FOOD PRODUCTION SYSTEM

NEW TRANSPORTATION STRUCTURE_H-LINE TRAIN SYSTEM

Existing Train Line

Planned Train Line

O O O Main City Stations

The train system is the key to future national planning in North Korea. This corridor is connecting from the end of South Korea to Russia, China, and European countries. The H-line is made up of the two vertical train lines along the North Korean coastline and one line connecting the two in the middle.

This H-line is stitching four economic hubs with eight main cities in the country; Pyongyang, Nampo, Sinuiju, Geasung, Rason, Chongjin, Hamhung, and Wonsan. Because of the connection to Seoul, which is the capital of South Korea, and China the west part of H-line would have lots of potential to be stronger.

This transit corridor is a fundamental framework of H-city and a catalyst for future developments in constructing a megaregion.

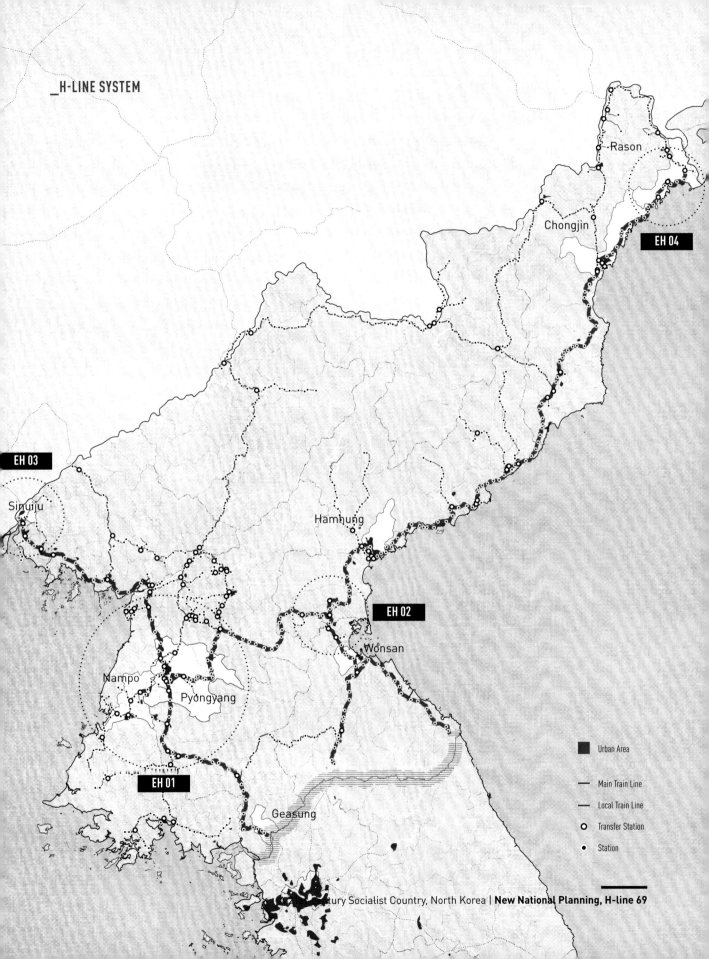

_H-LINE SYSTEM

EH 04

Rason

Chongjin

EH 03

Sinuiju

Hamhung

EH 02

Wŏnsan

Nampo

Pyŏngyang

EH 01

Geasung

Urban Area

Main Train Line

Local Train Line

○ Transfer Station

• Station

...tury Socialist Country, North Korea | **New National Planning, H-Line 69**

CURRENT URBANIZED AREA
25,367,910
Current Population in North Korea

82.9 % in 2010
Urbanization level in South Korea

60.2 % in 2010
Urbanization level in North Korea

**PREDICTED POPULATION MOVEMENT
AFTER ECONOMIC TRANSITION**

26,495,618 by 2040
Predicted Population in North Korea

After their economic transition, the H-line will start to be activated, and lots of people will move looking for jobs within the country or even from outside. This change will affect the population distribution of North Korea entirely. The predicted population of the country is 26,495,618 by 2040, which is not much different than the number in 2012, which was 24,589,122. However, this number will be concentrated along the H-line, especially toward the western part of H-city.

This change will affect urbanization too. The urbanization level of South Korea is 82.9%, which is 22.7% higher than North Korea. If this country is urbanized more, the area will be along H-line, too, like the population movement.

Based on the assumptions, the new density map is built.

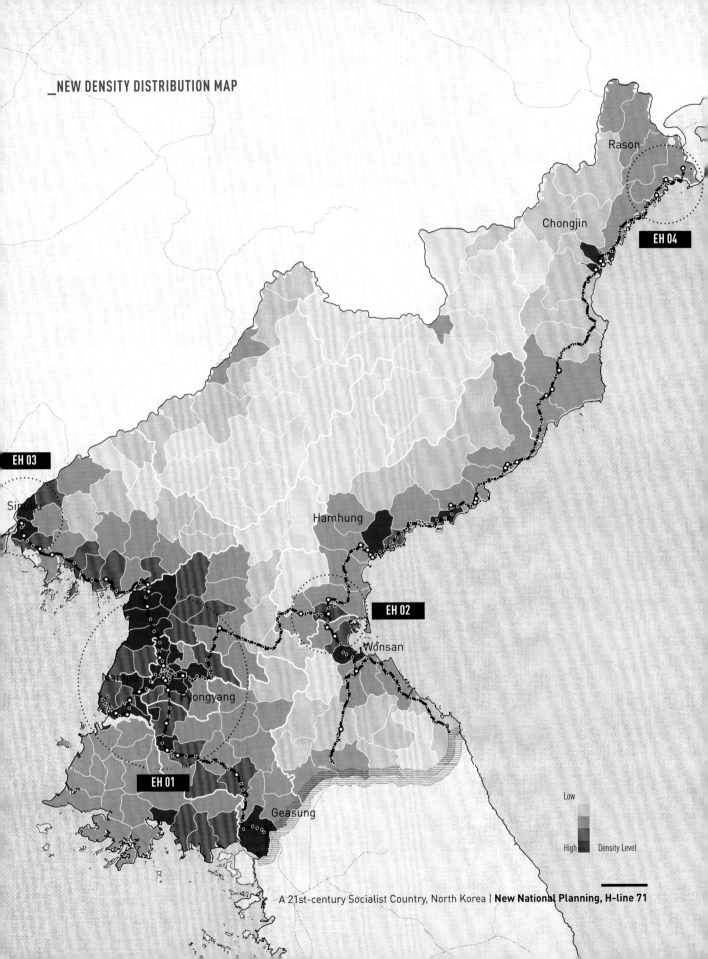

_NEW DENSITY DISTRIBUTION MAP

Rason

Chongjin

EH 04

EH 03

Sinuiju

Hamhung

EH 02

Wonsan

Manpo

Pyongyang

EH 01

Geasung

Low

High   Density Level

A 21st-century Socialist Country, North Korea | **New National Planning, H-line 71**

NEW ENERGY RESOURCE_WIND FARM

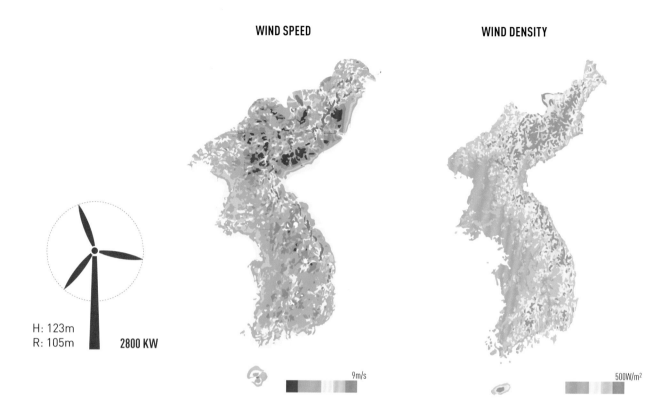

WIND SPEED

WIND DENSITY

9m/s

500W/m²

H: 123m
R: 105m
2800 KW

5,000,000 KW by 2044
Green Energy Future Plan in North Korea

1,785 Wind Power Plants
To Achieve 5,000,000 KW

150 m
Minimum Interval

270 km
For 1,785 Wind Power Plants

This country is suffering from an energy shortage, and even they are using coal mostly, which is not sustainable. Therefore, it is necessary to provide a stable supply of energy systems. Among various green energy options, the most suitable and realistic choice is a wind farm.
Furthermore, according to the wind speed and density map, the areas along the mountain range are appropriate for wind farms.
Is this energy spine enough to serve the country? Based on the Green Energy Future Plan done by the North Korean government, they are planning to generate 5,000,000 kW by 2044. This number means there will be 1,785 wind power plants, requiring 270km. The energy spine is 450km in length which is longer than 270km. This energy can be delivered directly to the east side of H-city through local train lines.
North Korea needs financial support for initial installation, but the combination of a hydro-electric power plant and wind farm can be a sustainable energy source.

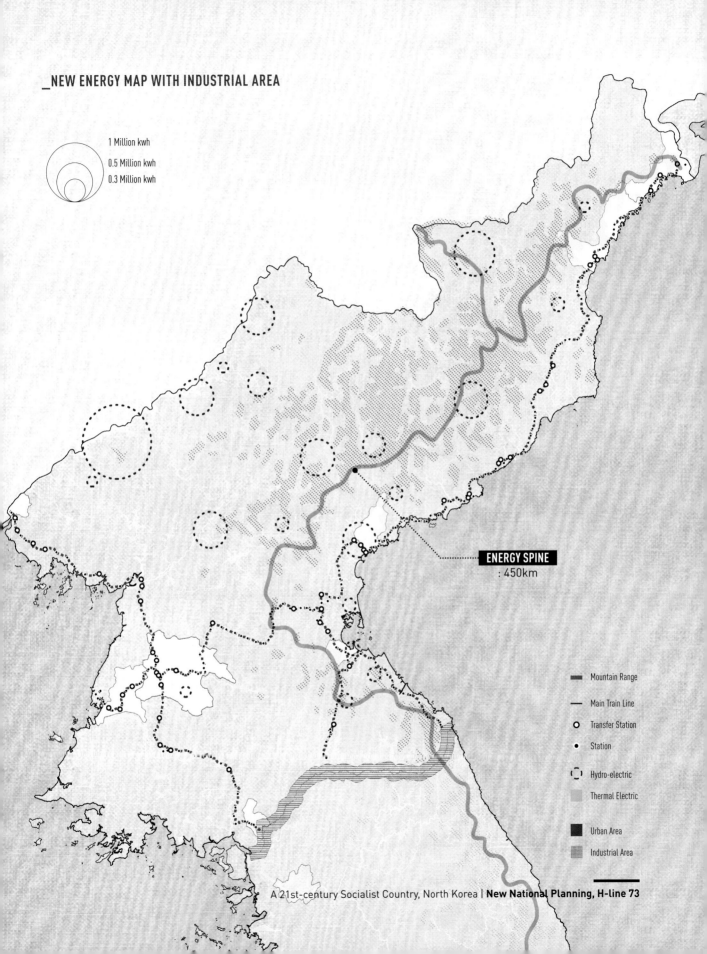

_NEW ENERGY MAP WITH INDUSTRIAL AREA

1 Million kwh
0.5 Million kwh
0.3 Million kwh

ENERGY SPINE
: 450km

Mountain Range

Main Train Line

○ Transfer Station

● Station

Hydro-electric

Thermal Electric

Urban Area

Industrial Area

A 21st-century Socialist Country, North Korea | New National Planning, H-line 73

NEW FOOD SYSTEM_ALPINE AGRICULTURE

FOOD DISTRIBUTION SYSTEM

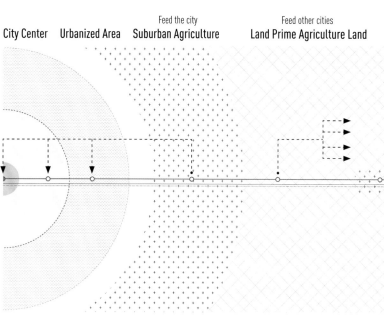

City Center   Urbanized Area   Feed the city
Suburban Agriculture   Feed other cities
Land Prime Agriculture Land

TO FEED A PERSON

2,300 Calories
For a Person per Day

1,850 m²
Land Needed per a person

5,537,900 Ha
New Productive Land in NK

29,934,595 People
Can be Feeded with 4,103,600 ha

MINIMUM LAND TO FEED ONE PERSON

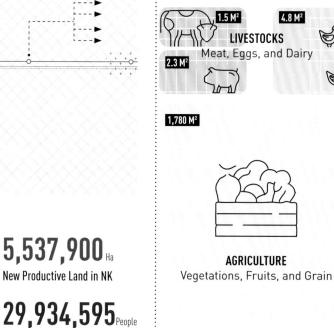

1,850 M²

62 M²

GRAIN / CORN
To Feed Livestocks

1.5 M²   4.8 M²

LIVESTOCKS
Meat, Eggs, and Dairy

2.3 M²

1,780 M²

AGRICULTURE
Vegetations, Fruits, and Grain

There are two big strategies for food production in North Korea. One is increasing efficiency in existing agriculture and grassland, and the other is introducing alpine agriculture. Fifty-one percent of North Korea is covered by mountains, but they do not need to make all the mountain areas agriculture hubs, just accessible for H-line and local train lines. This alpine area allows for 825,500 ha of potential agricultural land.

The minimum land requirement to feed just one person is 1,850 sqm and the overall productive land area in North Korea is 5,537,900 ha with existing and new alpine agriculture land. This area can feed 29,934,595 people, which is more than the predicted population in 2040. Furthermore, to increase the efficiency of the food distribution system, encouraging suburban areas to feed the city and concentrating on the prime agriculture land for production can solve the food shortage in the country.

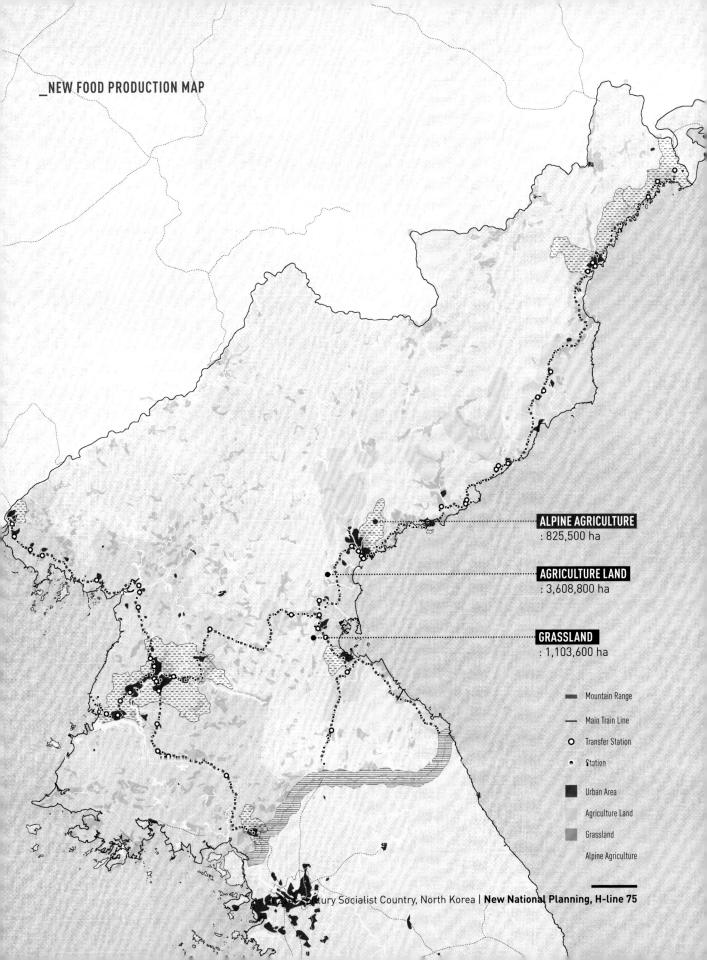

_NEW FOOD PRODUCTION MAP

ALPINE AGRICULTURE
: 825,500 ha

AGRICULTURE LAND
: 3,608,800 ha

GRASSLAND
: 1,103,600 ha

Mountain Range

Main Train Line

○ Transfer Station

• Station

Urban Area

Agriculture Land

Grassland

Alpine Agriculture

...tury Socialist Country, North Korea | **New National Planning, H-line 75**

NEW INDUSTRIAL STRUCTURE_

PRIMARY INDUSTRY	SECONDARY INDUSTRY	TERTIARY INDUSTRY
Farming Forestry Mining Fishing	Light Industry Heavy Industry	Education Finance Business Entertainment Professional Service

Light Industry

	Food	Clothes	Leather	Timber/Pulp	Publication	
Market	-	X	O	X	-	
Un-experienced Labor	O	-	-	O	X	
Experienced Labor	X	X	X	X	X	
Railway / Road	O	O	O	O	-	
Port	X	X	-	O	X	
Energy	X	O	O	X	X	O : High
Industrial Water	O	O	X	X	X	- : Medium
Resource	X	X	X	-	X	X : Low

Heavy Industry

	Chemistry	Rubber/Plastic	Glass/Cement	Steel/Metal	Mechanic	Computer	Electric	Automobile
Market	X	X	X	X	X	X	X	X
Un-experienced Labor	X	X	X	O	X	X	X	-
Experienced Labor	O	X	X	X	X	X	-	O
Railway / Road	X	X	-	O	O	O	O	-
Port	X	X	-	-	X	X	X	-
Energy	O	O	O	-	-	-	-	O
Industrial Water	O	O	X	-	X	X	X	O
Resource	X	-	-	-	X	X	X	O

The industry structure in North Korea is is their primary concentration, and tertiary is just being established and concentrated in the Pyongyang area. Therefore, the strategy here is to encourage secondary industries based on existing conditions and new national planning and locating centers for important tertiary sectors such as finance and business.

The distribution of these industries is based on the table above. The criteria are about how each factor is essential for each sector. Pyongyang is the center of tertiary industries in North Korea. It is a core of business and finance. Furthermore, because of the accessibility to energy, most of the heavy industries are concentrated on the eastern side of H-city. Currently, Geasung is an exclusive industrial zone to corporate with South Korea. This city can be a real center of technical exchange between two Koreas.

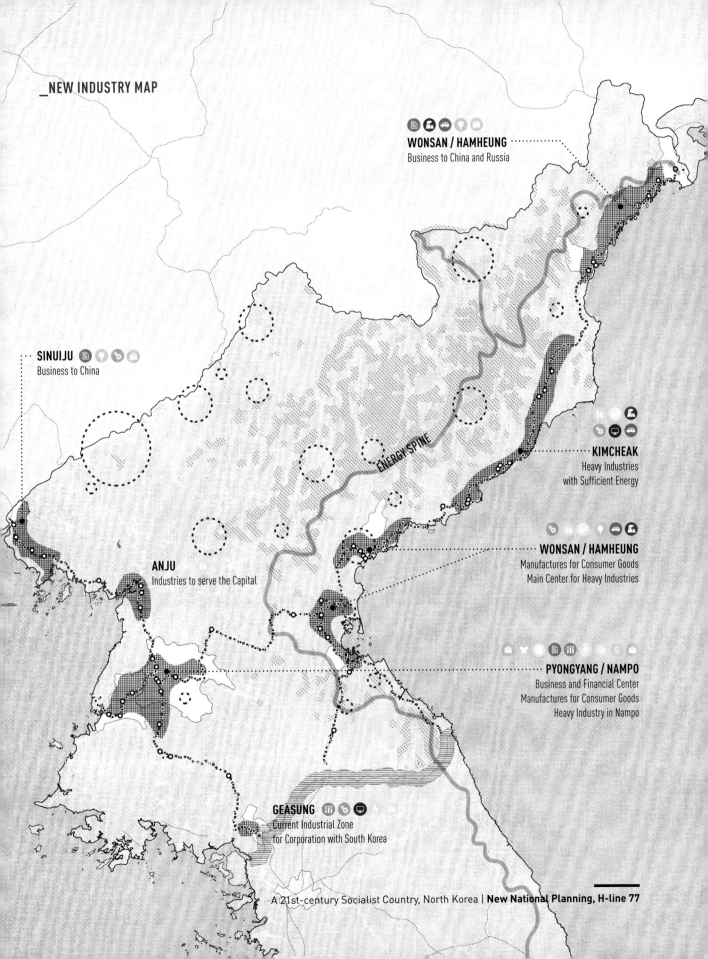

_NEW INDUSTRY MAP

WONSAN / HAMHEUNG
Business to China and Russia

SINUIJU
Business to China

KIMCHEAK
Heavy Industries
with Sufficient Energy

ENERGY SPINE

WONSAN / HAMHEUNG
Manufactures for Consumer Goods
Main Center for Heavy Industries

ANJU
Industries to serve the Capital

PYONGYANG / NAMPO
Business and Financial Center
Manufactures for Consumer Goods
Heavy Industry in Nampo

GEASUNG
Current Industrial Zone
for Corporation with South Korea

A 21st-century Socialist Country, North Korea | **New National Planning, H-line 77**

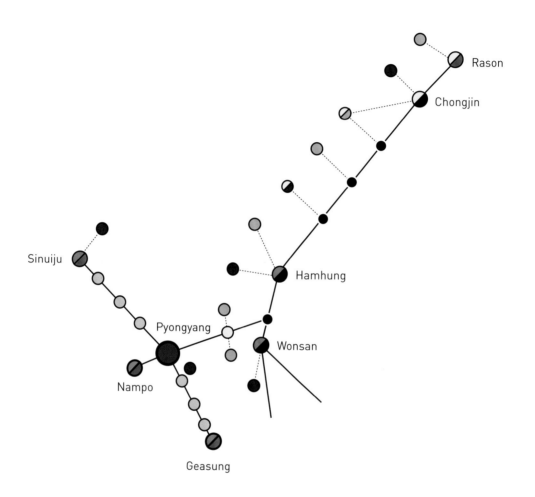

Rason

Chongjin

Sinuiju

Hamhung

Pyongyang

Wonsan

Nampo

Geasung

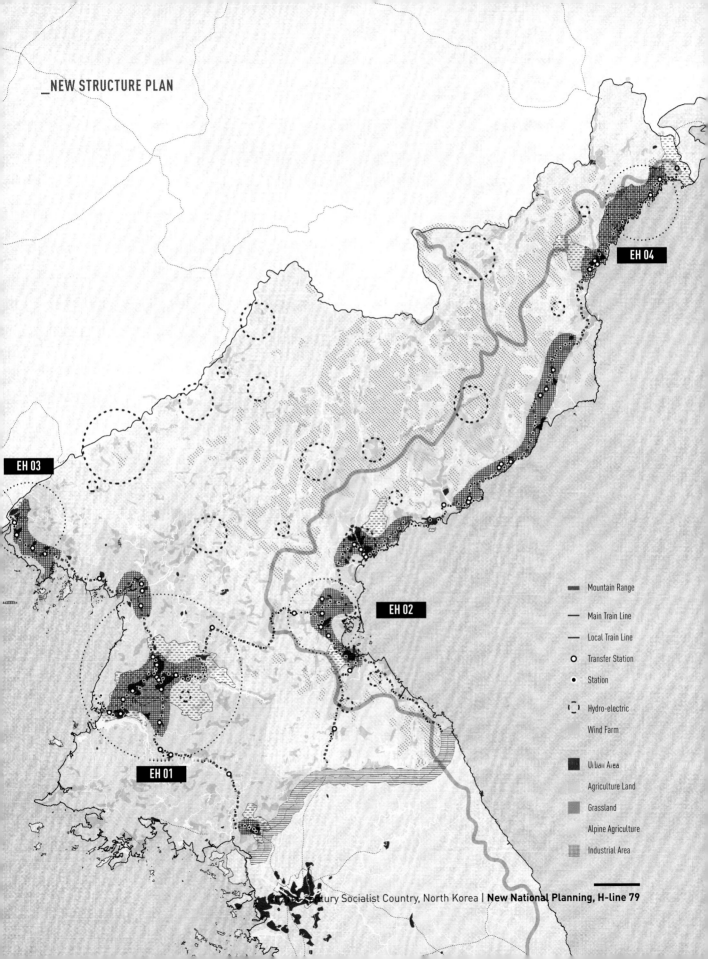

_NEW STRUCTURE PLAN

EH 04

EH 03

EH 02

EH 01

Mountain Range

Main Train Line

Local Train Line

○ Transfer Station

• Station

Hydro-electric

Wind Farm

Urban Area

Agriculture Land

Grassland

Alpine Agriculture

Industrial Area

...tury Socialist Country, North Korea | **New National Planning, H-line 79**

SECTIONS_WITH H-CITY PLANNING

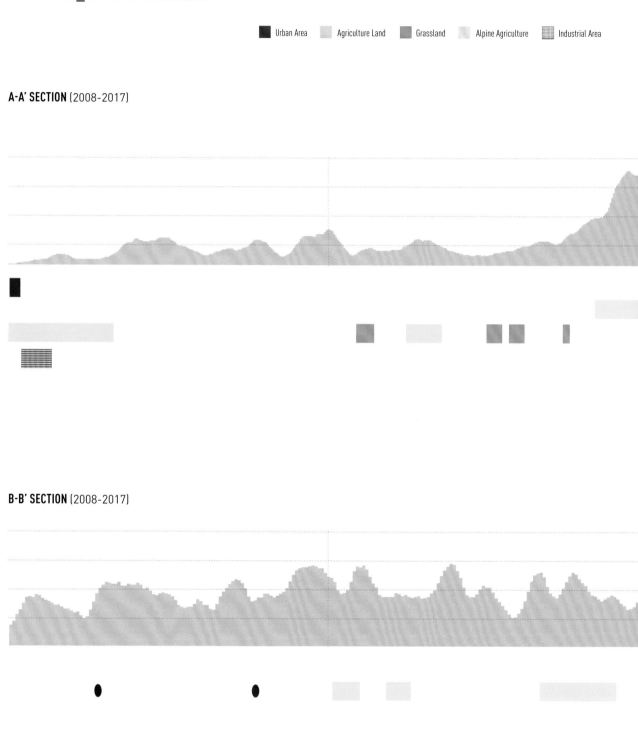

■ Urban Area   ░ Agriculture Land   ▓ Grassland   ░ Alpine Agriculture   ▦ Industrial Area

A-A' SECTION (2008-2017)

B-B' SECTION (2008-2017)

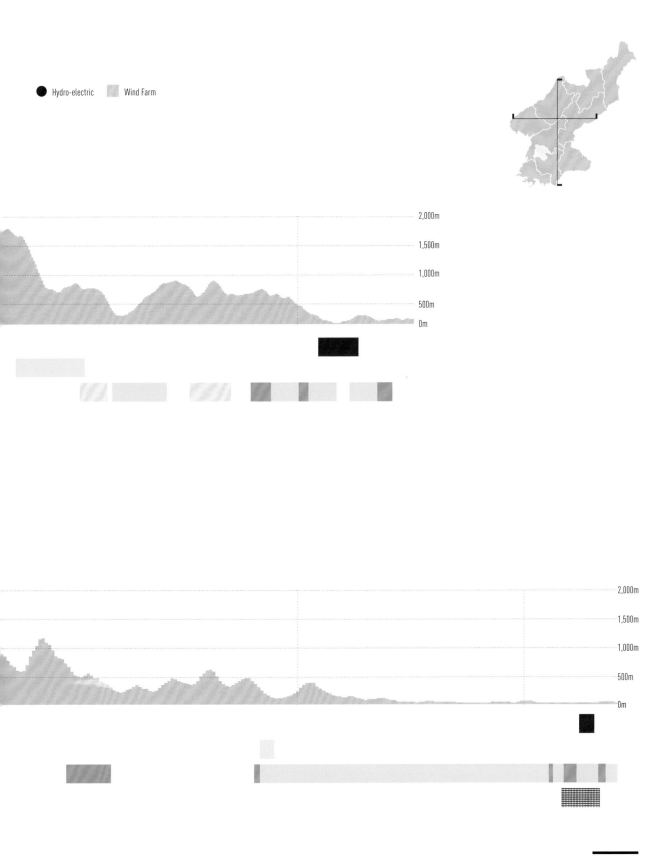

Hydro-electric   Wind Farm

2,000m
1,500m
1,000m
500m
0m

2,000m
1,500m
1,000m
500m
0m

H-city
and the H-stations

3

1 Main Station
2 Urban Station
3 Uuburban Station
4 Agricultural Town Station
5 Industrial Town Station
6 Village Station
7 Empty Station

H-city and the Stations

The composition of H-line

Along H-line, there are six types of train stations excluding empty stations where there is nothing around. These include the central station, urban station, suburban station, agricultural town station, industrial town station, and village station. These types are based on the new national planning and determined by the station and the location of their urban context. There are 7 main stations, 21 urban stations, 31 suburban stations, 41 agricultural town stations, 21 industrial town station, 113 village stations, and 18 empty stations along H-line.

The east side of the line is the central part connecting North Korea to South Korea and China. The main stations on this side are Sinuiju, Pyongyang, and Geasung. Pyongyang is the center of the country. In every part of the economy, this city will be the core. In the case of Sinuiju, it is a gateway to China actively exchanging goods and people. Geasung has lots of potential to receive technical help from South Korea. The south can be beneficial with labor, and the north can gain the skills needed.

The west side of the H-line is an extended linear area between the mountains and the ocean. It is a combination of energy, industries, and some amount of productive land. The heavy industries and ports along H-line bring jobs and incomes to the country.

The middle part is not only the connection between the two sides of transit corridors but also the closest area to enjoy the mountains from the cities and connects the two main ports in the country.

TYPOLOGIES OF TRAIN STATION_IN H-CITY

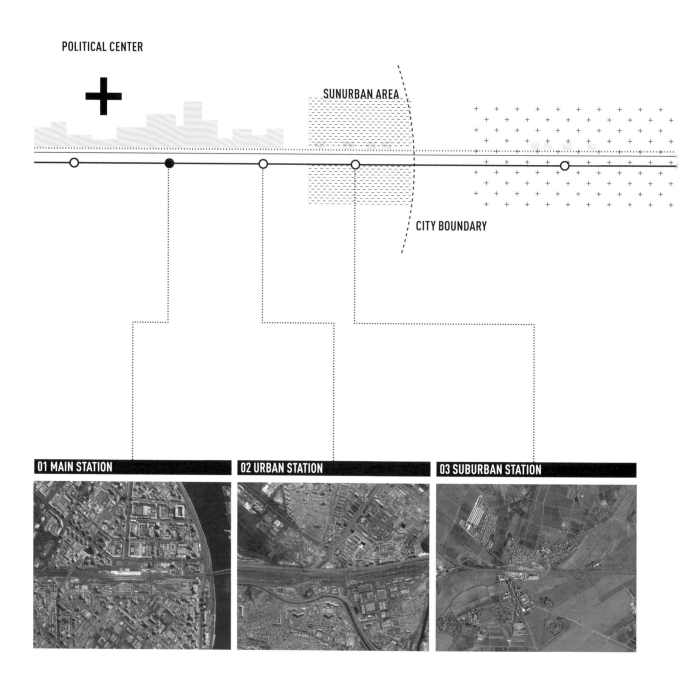

POLITICAL CENTER

SUNURBAN AREA

CITY BOUNDARY

01 MAIN STATION

02 URBAN STATION

03 SUBURBAN STATION

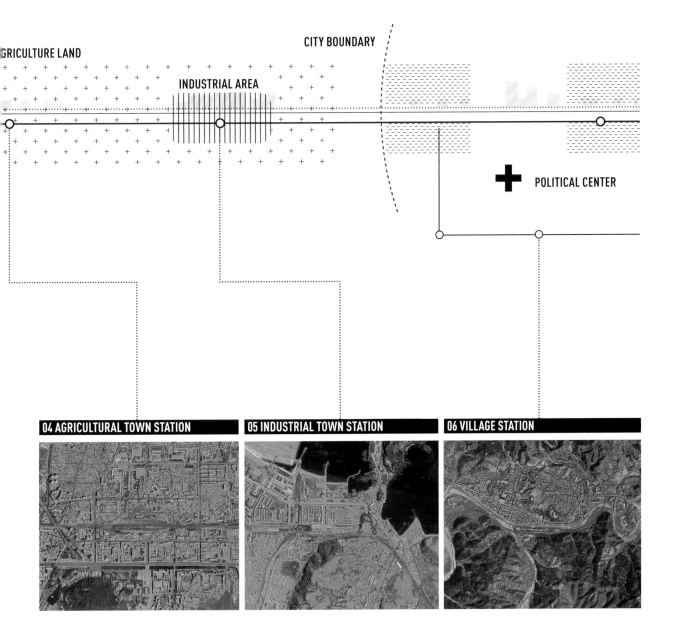

AGRICULTURE LAND

CITY BOUNDARY

INDUSTRIAL AREA

POLITICAL CENTER

04 AGRICULTURAL TOWN STATION

05 INDUSTRIAL TOWN STATION

06 VILLAGE STATION

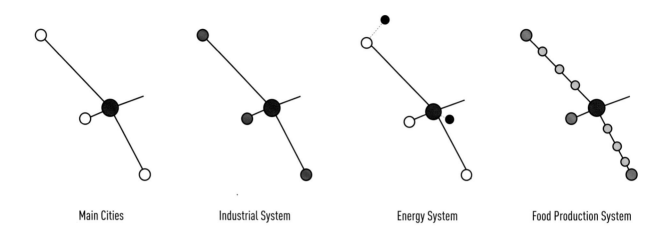

| Main Cities | Industrial System | Energy System | Food Production System |

M: MAIN STATION **U**: URBAN STATION **S**: SUBURBAN STATION **A**: AGRICULTURAL TOWN STATION **I**: INDUSTRIAL TOWN STATION **V**: VILLAGE STATION **E**: EMPTY STATION

CATALOGUE OF STATIONS

STATION	M	U	S	A	I	V	E
Gang-an		v					
Sinuiju Cheongnyeon	v						
Nam-sinuiju		v					
Rakwon		v					
Yongchon				v			
Yongju					v		
Neajung					v		
Yeomju			v				
Dongrim					v		
Chonggang					v		
Sonchon				v			
Roha					v		
Kwaksan			v				
Hadan					v		
Jeongju Cheongnyeon			v				
Goeup					v		
Unam					v		
Unjeon			v				
Meangjungri					v		
Chongcheongang						v	
Sinanju				v			

STATION	M	U	S	A	I	V	E
Deakyo						v	
Munduck			v				
Sukcheon			v				
Eopa					v		
Suck-am			v				
Sun-an			v				
Galli			v				
San-um			v				
Seopo		v					
Pyongyang Classification		v					
Western Pyongyang		v					
Pyongyang	v						
Deadonggang		v			v		
Ryeokpo			v				
Chunghwa			v				
Hukgyo					v		
Gandong						v	
Hwangju			v				
Chimchon					v		
Jungbangri					v		
Sariwon			v				

STATION	M	U	S	A	I	V	E
Eastern Sariwon		v					
Bongsan			v				
Chong-gea						v	
Hongsu						v	
Munmu						v	
Sohung						v	
Sinmak				v			
Mulgea						v	
Pyongsan				v			
Teabeaksansung							v
Hanpo						v	
Kumchon				v			
Geajung						v	
Yeohyun						v	
Keeping						v	
Geasung	v						
Sonha		v					
Bongdong						v	
Panmun			v				

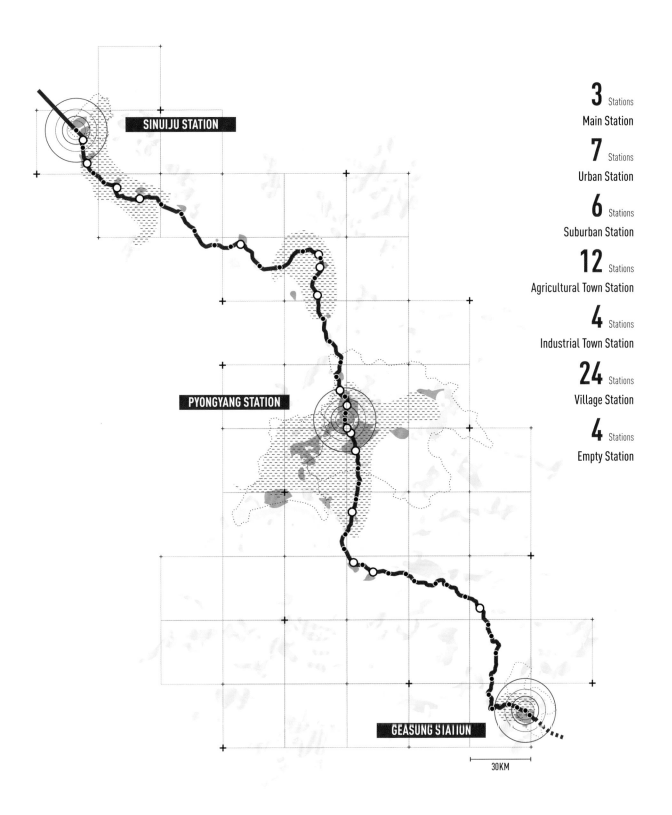

3 Stations
Main Station

7 Stations
Urban Station

6 Stations
Suburban Station

12 Stations
Agricultural Town Station

4 Stations
Industrial Town Station

24 Stations
Village Station

4 Stations
Empty Station

SINUIJU STATION

PYONGYANG STATION

GEASUNG STATION

30KM

EAST PART OF H-CITY_WITH MAIN STATIONS

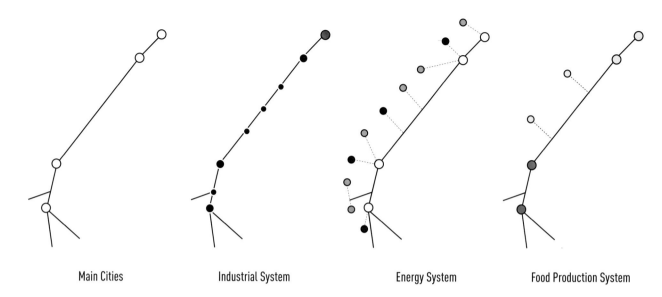

Main Cities   Industrial System   Energy System   Food Production System

M: MAIN STATION **U**: URBAN STATION **S**: SUBURBAN STATION **A**: AGRICULTURAL TOWN STATION **I**: INDUSTRIAL TOWN STATION **V**: VILLAGE STATION **E**: EMPTY STATION

CATALOGUE OF STATIONS

STATION	M	U	S	A	I	V	E
Tumangang						v	
Guryeongpo							v
Ungsang						v	
Eastern Sonbong			v				
Sonbong			v				
Kwangok		v		v			
Rajin	v						
Myongho							v
Huchang						v	
Bangjin						v	
Northern Raksan						v	
Gwanhea						v	
Same						v	
Buga						v	
Sagu							v
Injin						v	
Songwon						v	
Geumbaui				v			
Chong-am		v					
Chongjin		v					
Sunam	v						

STATION	M	U	S	A	I	V	E
Songpyong	v			v			
Southern Gangduck	v						
Ranam		v					
Sungam		v					
Seanggiryeong						v	
Kyongsong			v				
Ryonghyun						v	
Orang			v				
Odeajin						v	
Bongang						v	
Jomaksan						v	
Gekdong						v	
Samhyang			v				
Ryongdong						v	
Sangryongban						v	
Ryongban						v	
Neapo					v		
Myongcheon						v	
Onsupyong						v	
Geumsong						v	
Gilju				v			

STATION	M	U	S	A	I	V	E
Rodong						v	
Wonpyong						v	
Upduck						v	
Songsang						v	
Changbong						v	
Haksung					v		
Kinchaek					v		
Ssangryong						v	
Manchun						v	
Ilsin						v	
Ryongdea						v	
Yeoheajin						v	
Munam							v
Tanchon				v			
Obongri						v	
Sindanchon						v	
Kiam						v	
Gokgu						v	
Ssangam						v	

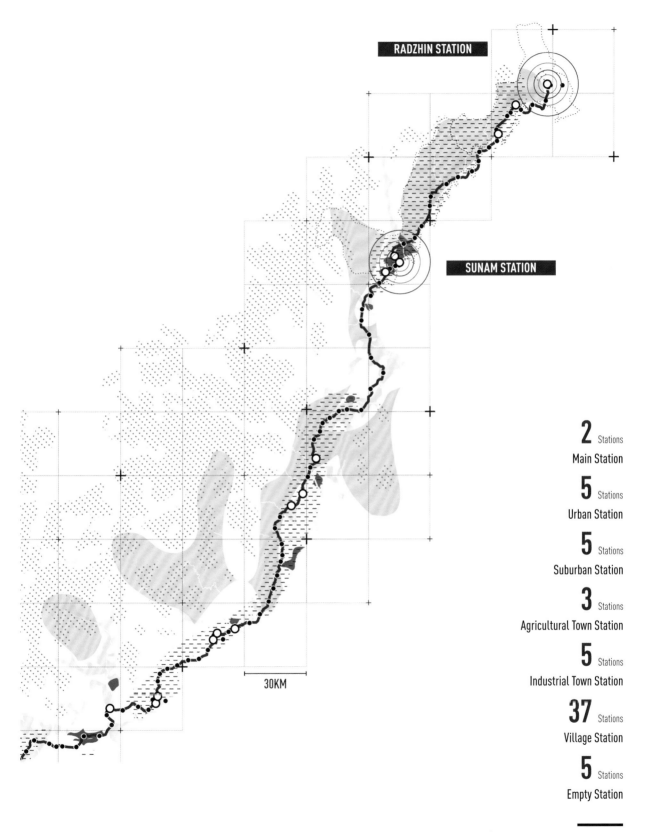

RADZHIN STATION

SUNAM STATION

30KM

2 Stations
Main Station

5 Stations
Urban Station

5 Stations
Suburban Station

3 Stations
Agricultural Town Station

5 Stations
Industrial Town Station

37 Stations
Village Station

5 Stations
Empty Station

M: MAIN STATION **U**: URBAN STATION **S**: SUBURBAN STATION **A**: AGRICULTURAL TOWN STATION **I**: INDUSTRIAL TOWN STATION **V**: VILLAGE STATION **E**: EMPTY STATION

CATALOGUE OF STATIONS

STATION	M	U	S	A	I	V	E
Riwon				v			
Songdan						v	
Yumbun							v
Jeongsan						v	
Rahong					v		
Gunja						v	
Geosan						v	
Keongan						v	
Sinbukcheong						v	
Sokhu			v				
Kangsanri						v	
Yanghwa			v				
Sinpo					v		
Yukteadong			v				
Pungeo						v	
Jungho						v	
Unpo						v	
Kyeongpo						v	
Hongwon			v				
Ryong-un						v	
Samho						v	
Rasan							v
Seapori						v	
Ryeoho					v		
Sinjung							v
Major						v	
Seoho		v					
Hongnam		v					
Janghonh			v				
Hamhung Classification		v					
Hamhung	v						
Juseo							v
Hamju			v				
Chongpyong			v				

STATION	M	U	S	A	I	V	E
Puphyong						v	
Sinsang				v			
Munbong							v
Wangjang				v			
Pompho						v	
Inhung				v			
Kumya				v			
Hyunhong						v	
Kowon				v			
Jeontan					v		
Ryongdam						v	
Okpyong						v	
Muncheon	v						
Dukwon			v				
Wonsan	v						
Galma		v					
Beahwa					v		
Anyone					v		
Namsan						v	
Gwangmyeong				v			
Ryongjiwon						v	
Kosan				v			
Nakcheon						v	
Sambang						v	
Sepo Cheong-nyeon				v			
Sungsan						v	
Gumbulang						v	
Rimok						v	
Bokgea						v	
Pyonggang				v			
Ogye						v	
Sangum						v	

STATION	M	U	S	A	I	V	E
Dongjungho			v				
Myonggo						v	
Geombonggang						v	
Sijungho			v				
Tongchon			v	v			
Donghea			v				
Ryeomsung						v	
Dupo			v	v			
Gosung			v	v			
Geomgangsan Cheongnyeon						v	
Gamho							v

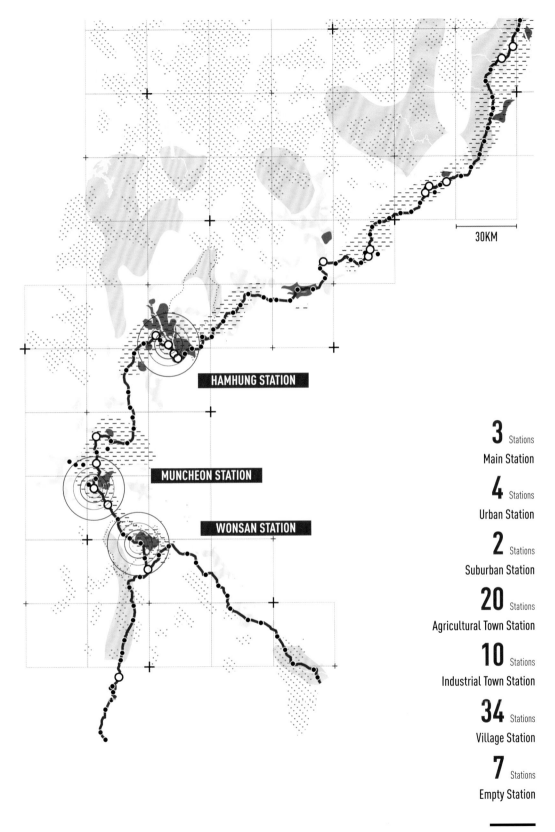

HAMHUNG STATION

MUNCHEON STATION

WONSAN STATION

30KM

3 Stations
Main Station

4 Stations
Urban Station

2 Stations
Suburban Station

20 Stations
Agricultural Town Station

10 Stations
Industrial Town Station

34 Stations
Village Station

7 Stations
Empty Station

MIDDLE PART OF H-CITY_WITH MAIN STATIONS

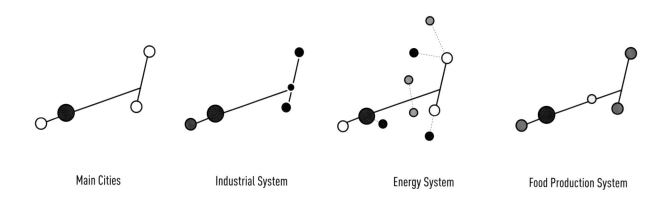

Main Cities   Industrial System   Energy System   Food Production System

M: MAIN STATION **U**: URBAN STATION **S**: SUBURBAN STATION **A**: AGRICULTURAL TOWN STATION **I**: INDUSTRIAL TOWN STATION **V**: VILLAGE STATION **E**: EMPTY STATION

CATALOGUE OF STATIONS

STATION	M	U	S	A	I	V	E
Onchon				v			
Guisung				v			
Rosang					v		
Hwado				v			
Western Gwangryang				v			
Eastern Gwangryang				v			
Sinryeongri		v					
Dukdong		v					
Sinnampo		v					
Nampo	v						
Galchon		v					
Ryonggang		v					
Ganseo		v		v			
Gangson		v		v			
Deapyong		v					
Chilgol		v					
Potonggang		v					
Pyongyang	v						
Deadonggang		v					
Eastern Pyongyang		v					
Songsin		v					
Mirim	v						
Chongryong		v					
Ripsungri		v					
Seonghori		v		v			
Mandalri		v					
Hwachon		v					
Songga		v					
Samdeong		v					
Heoksuk		v					
Sukreum		v					
Gangdong		v					
Beakwon					v		
Sungchon					v		
Samduk					v		
Sinsungchon					v		
Geoheung					v		
Changrim					v		
Sinyang					v		
Anpyong					v		
Jisu						v	
Yangduk			v				
Neadong							v
Suktang Onchon						v	
Geocha						v	
Chonyul						v	
Ungok						v	
Yoduk						v	
Toryong						v	
Munpyong						v	
Sungnea						v	
Dunjeon						v	
Palhong						v	
Chukjeon						v	
Midun						v	
Banghwa				v			

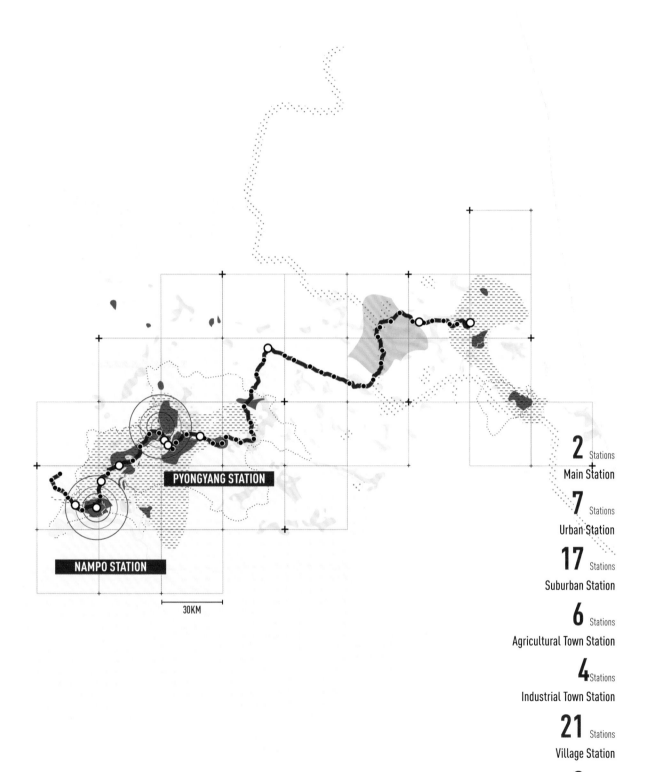

PYONGYANG STATION

NAMPO STATION

30KM

2 Stations
Main Station

7 Stations
Urban Station

17 Stations
Suburban Station

6 Stations
Agricultural Town Station

4 Stations
Industrial Town Station

21 Stations
Village Station

2 Stations
Empty Station

A 21st-century Socialist Country, North Korea | **H-city and the H-stations 95**

02

Based on the H-city plan,
there are six typologies
of train stations. The
six typologies each
have a different role
in the surroundings
and characteristics.
Understanding each
typology is critical to
making stations a catalyst
for the future.

The Typologies of H-stations

The characteristics of the six typologies

The six typologies of the stations in H-line have different characteristics. The hexagon with six primary elements shows these visually. Each one has six criteria to explain their features. The factors about the stations themselves are the size, composition of the station, and the width of the train tracks. Other factors that describe their urban features are the surrounding density, the area of public space, and the role of the station within a city.

The main station is geometrically and symbolically the core of the city and the country. It has the most significant number in station size and composition but not in the width of the train tracks. In the case of urban factors, it has the highest number in all three elements.

The urban station is a sub-center of a city. It is following after or before the main station. It has a less representative role but more daily life related. Because the main station is too busy to handle distribution, this typology is taking over partially, causing it to have the most extensive train track area.

The suburban station is located in productive land within the jurisdiction of a city. That means it is in the city area but not urbanized. Therefore, most of the numbers are small.

The fourth and fifth typologies are the agricultural and industrial town stations. They have similar features except for the density and the role of the station. It is the center of smaller cities, but each one is concentrated in agriculture or industries.

The last one is the village station. This type is located in a rural area with the lowest density. The train is the only public space and public transportation in the town.

INTRODUCTION_ THE MATRIX FOR THE TRAIN STATIONS

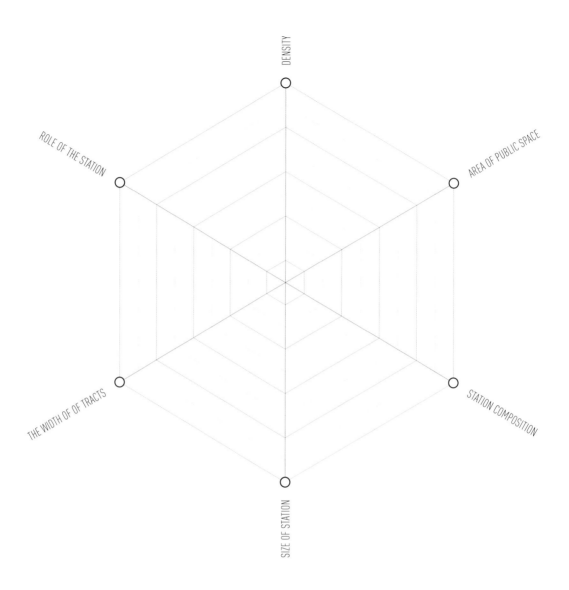

The hexagon represents six essential elements that determine the characteristics of the stations, and each factor has its own rating system. The first one indicates density rated from 0 to 4.5, which means the floor-area ratio. The next one is the area of public space, or wheth-

er a station has it or not. The third presents how many elements the station has in its composition, such as a concealed platform or a connection to other public transportation. The fourth provides the size of these stations. The fifth is the width of tracks, which further indicates out

how many tracks there are. The last describes the role of the station in the surrounding area; this role can be presented as a town center or special destination area for vacations.

DENSITY Floor Area Ratio	AREA OF PUBLIC SPACE Acres	STATION COMPOSITION	SIZE OF STATION Acres	THE WIDTH OF TRACKS Meters / Feet	ROLE OF STATION
4.5	10	All-in-one Building	5.0		City Center
4		Connected Other Public Transportation	1.0	80m (260ft)	
3.5	1	Public Space	0.5		Town Center
3.0		Protected Connection over Train Tracks	0.1	60m (195ft)	
2.5		Attached Other Programs	0.08		Special Destination
2.0		Station Building	0.06	40m (130ft)	
1.5		Covered Paltform	0.04		Neighborhood Center
1.0		Platform	0.02	20m (65ft)	
0.5		Train Tracks	0.01	10m (30ft)	Transportation
0	0	Nothing	0	0	Nothing

Extreme

High

Medium

Low

The main stations are the central train stations in a big city. This is a gateway to enter a city from outside, therefore, its role in the country is significant. It should be have the highest density in North Korea. This type usually has an iconic or symbolic elevation attached to substantial public spaces.

The size of the station is more significant than any other and is tied to other programs such as commercial or civic. However, the width of the train tracks here would not be the largest because this station is not a center for industrial or transit movement that requires heavy train traffic.

There are only eight stations in this category along H-line, which means they should remain as an iconic or symbolic station as they can represent the country or the cities.

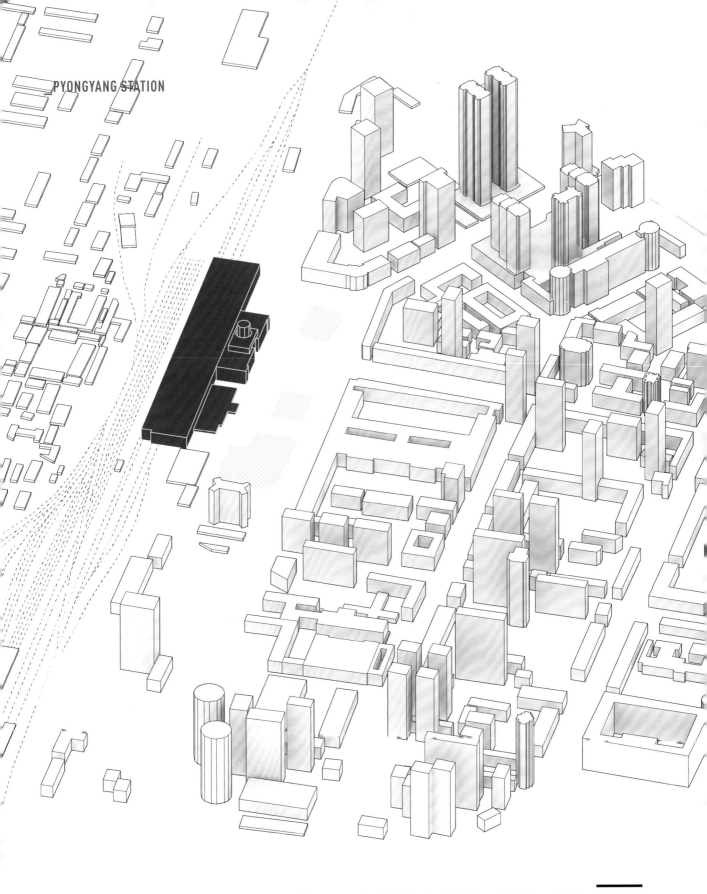

PYONGYANG STATION

01 MAIN STATION_SAMPLES

PYONGYANG STATION

DENSITY — EXTREME

AREA OF PUBLIC SPACE — 8.5 ACRES

STATION COMPOSITION — 10 ELEMENTS

SIZE OF STATION — 5 ACRES

WIDTH OF TRACTS — 115 M (377FT)

ROLE OF STATION — CITY CENTER

SINUIJU STATION

DENSITY — EXTREME

AREA OF PUBLIC SPACE — 14 ACRES

STATION COMPOSITION — 9 ELEMENTS

SIZE OF STATION — 5.7 ACRES

WIDTH OF TRACTS — 77 M (250FT)

ROLE OF STATION — CITY CENTER

CHUNGJIN STATION

DENSITY — EXTREME

AREA OF PUBLIC SPACE — 6.5 ACRES

STATION COMPOSITION — 8 ELEMENTS

SIZE OF STATION — 4.5 ACRES

WIDTH OF TRACTS — 86 M (280FT)

ROLE OF STATION — CITY CENTER

NAMPO STATION

DENSITY — HIGH

AREA OF PUBLIC SPACE — 9.7 ACRES

STATION COMPOSITION — 8 ELEMENTS

SIZE OF STATION — 0.4 ACRES

WIDTH OF TRACTS — 77 M (250FT)

ROLE OF STATION — CITY CENTER

RAJIN STATION

DENSITY — HIGH

AREA OF PUBLIC SPACE — 3.15 ACRES

STATION COMPOSITION — 8 ELEMENTS

SIZE OF STATION — 0.6 ACRES

WIDTH OF TRACTS — 54 M (176FT)

ROLE OF STATION — CITY CENTER

SUNAM STATION

DENSITY — MEDIUM

AREA OF PUBLIC SPACE — 1.5 ACRES

STATION COMPOSITION — 8 ELEMENTS

SIZE OF STATION — 0.15 ACRES

WIDTH OF TRACTS — 80 M (260FT)

ROLE OF STATION — CITY CENTER

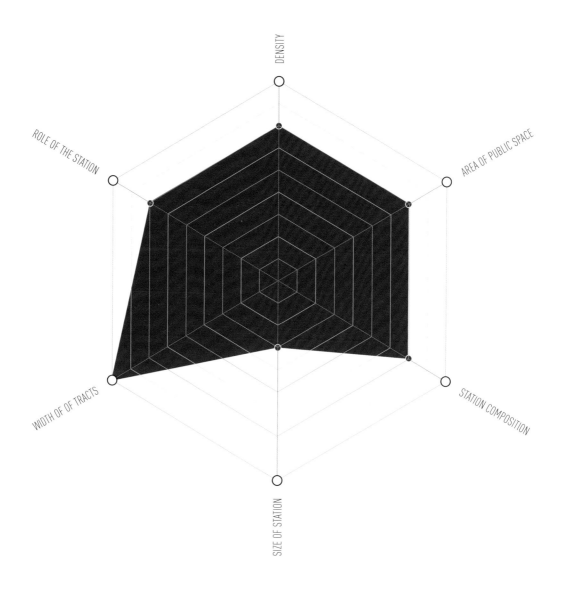

The urban stations are located within the jurisdiction of a big city and surrounded by a relatively higher density. Usually, they come before or after the main station, acting as a subcenter for a city or sometimes located along the edge of an urbanized area. It has public space in front of the station and is smaller than that of the main stations, but the composition is similar. The urban station typology has smaller station sizes but with more train tracks serving the surrounding industries. If the main stations are seen as gateways to cities, then the urban stations would act as centers for the daily lives of citizens, providing lots of jobs in factories.

Therefore, this type is more tied to the citizen who is commuting and spending time around the stations.

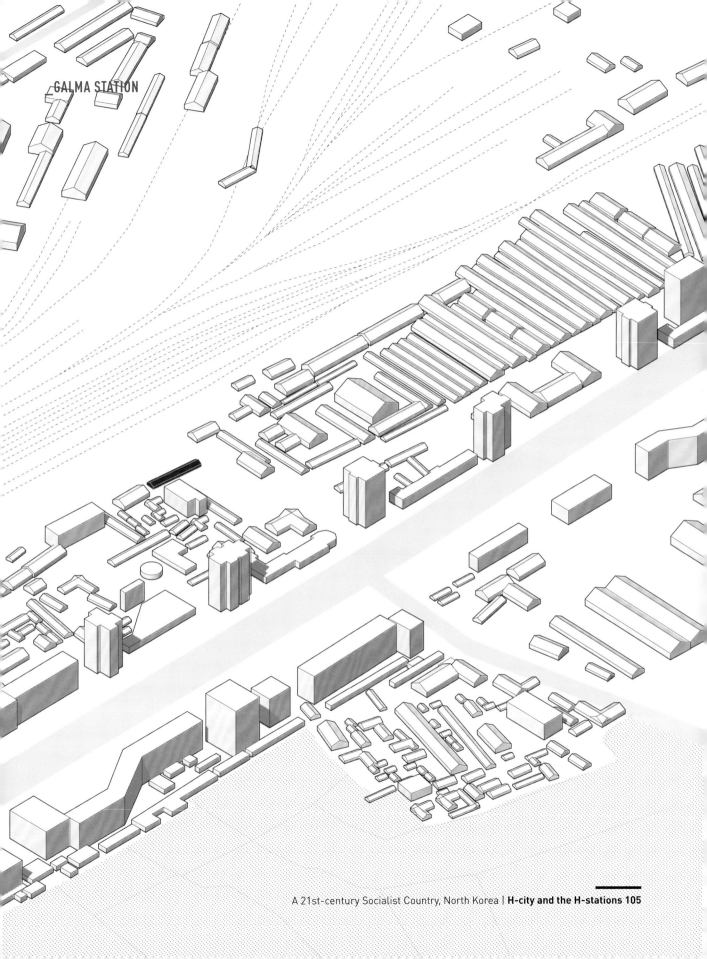

GALMA STATION

GALMA STATION

DENSITY	MEDIUM
AREA OF PUBLIC SPACE	0.7 ACRES
STATION COMPOSITION	8 ELEMENTS
SIZE OF STATION	0.1 ACRES
WIDTH OF TRACTS	145 M (475FT)
ROLE OF STATION	TOWN CENTER

DEADONGGANG STATION

DENSITY	MEDEUM
AREA OF PUBLIC SPACE	0.7 ACRES
STATION COMPOSITION	5 ELEMENTS
SIZE OF STATION	0.2 ACRES
WIDTH OF TRACTS	105 M (340FT)
ROLE OF STATION	TOWN CENTER

CHONGJIN STATION

DENSITY	MEDIUM
AREA OF PUBLIC SPACE	3.8 ACRES
STATION COMPOSITION	8 ELEMENTS
SIZE OF STATION	0.45 ACRES
WIDTH OF TRACTS	145 M (475FT)
ROLE OF STATION	TOWN CENTER

WESTERN PYONGYANG STATION

DENSITY	EXTREME
AREA OF PUBLIC SPACE	6.8 ACRES
STATION COMPOSITION	8 ELEMENTS
SIZE OF STATION	0.5 ACRES
WIDTH OF TRACTS	120 M (390FT)
ROLE OF STATION	TOWN CENTER

HAMHUNG CLASSIFICATION STATION

DENSITY	MEDIUM
AREA OF PUBLIC SPACE	0 ACRES
STATION COMPOSITION	5 ELEMENTS
SIZE OF STATION	0.23 ACRES
WIDTH OF TRACTS	220M (720FT)
ROLE OF STATION	TOWN CENTER

GANG-AN STATION

DENSITY	MEDEUM
AREA OF PUBLIC SPACE	0 ACRES
STATION COMPOSITION	5 ELEMENTS
SIZE OF STATION	0.16 ACRES
WIDTH OF TRACTS	67 M (220FT)
ROLE OF STATION	TOWN CENTER

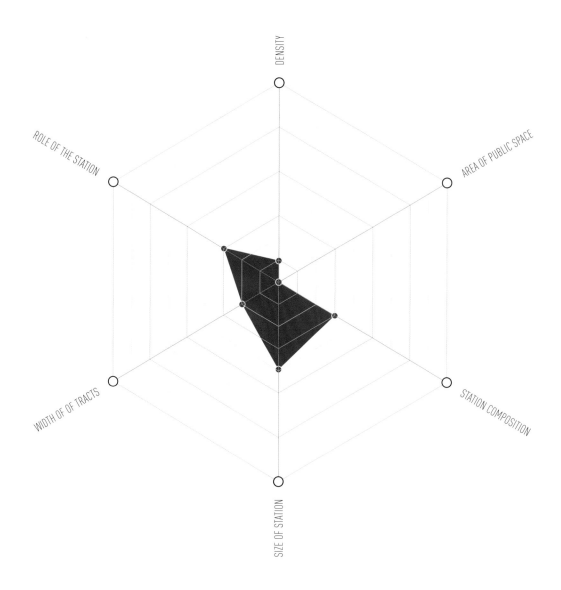

The suburban stations are located within a jurisdiction of a big city but outside of the urbanized area. This area is the center for food production that provides for its city, which is why it is surrounded by a lower density population and productive land. It does not have a public space attached, but this area is a neighborhood center. The composition of these stations is more straightforward than the previous two, which means it only has the station, open platform, train tracks, and connection to other public transportation.

Therefore, this type needs to be focused on food production and distribution, providing a central area for the neighborhood to gather and spend time together.

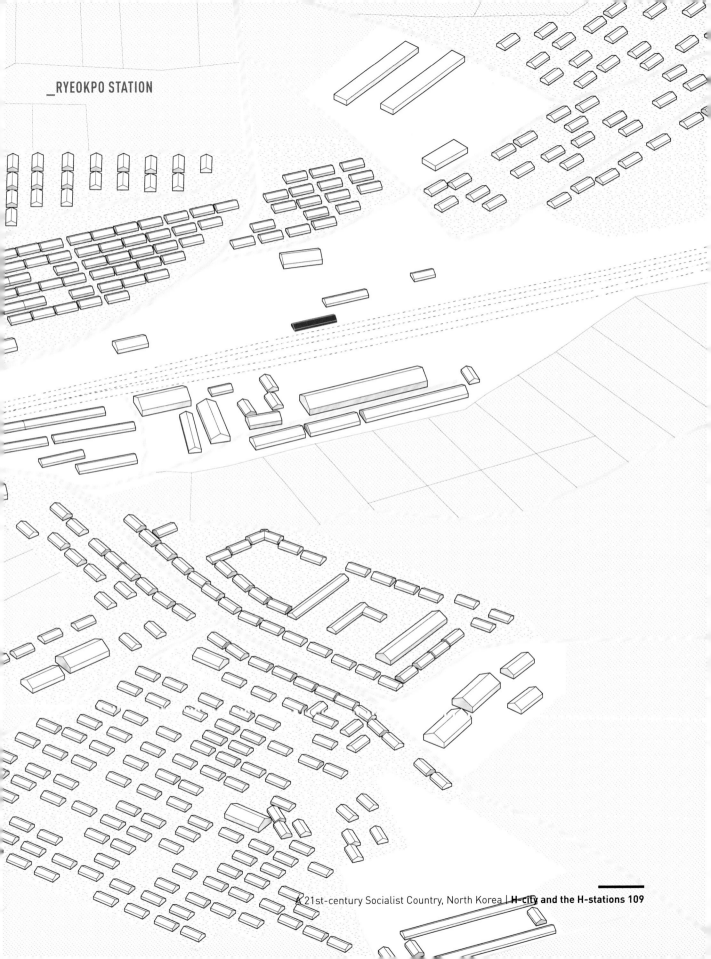

_RYEOKPO STATION

03 SUBURBAN STATION_SAMPLES

RYEOKPO STATION

DENSITY	LOW
AREA OF PUBLIC SPACE	0 ACRES
STATION COMPOSITION	3 ELEMENTS
SIZE OF STATION	0.09 ACRES
WIDTH OF TRACTS	30 M (100FT)
ROLE OF STATION	NEIGHBORHOOD CENTER

DUKDONG STATION

DENSITY	LOW
AREA OF PUBLIC SPACE	0 ACRES
STATION COMPOSITION	3 ELEMENTS
SIZE OF STATION	0.05 ACRES
WIDTH OF TRACTS	15 M (50FT)
ROLE OF STATION	NEIGHBORHOOD CENTER

OGYE STATION

DENSITY	LOW
AREA OF PUBLIC SPACE	0 ACRES
STATION COMPOSITION	3 ELEMENTS
SIZE OF STATION	0.08 ACRES
WIDTH OF TRACTS	15 M (50FT)
ROLE OF STATION	NEIGHBORHOOD CENTER

GALLI STATION

DENSITY | LOW
|||||||||||||

AREA OF PUBLIC SPACE | 2.3 ACRES
||||||||||||||||||||||||||||||||||||

STATION COMPOSITION | 5 ELEMENTS
|||||||||||||||||||||||||||

SIZE OF STATION | 0.25 ACRES
||||||||||||||||||||||||||||||||||||

WIDTH OF TRACTS | 115 M (370FT)
||||||||||||||||||||||||||||||||||||

ROLE OF STATION | NEIGHBORHOOD CENTER
|||||||||||||||||||||

SINRYEONGRI STATION

DENSITY | LOW
|||||||||||||

AREA OF PUBLIC SPACE | 0 ACRES

STATION COMPOSITION | 3 ELEMENTS
|||||||||||||||||

SIZE OF STATION | 0.05 ACRES
||||||||||||||||

WIDTH OF TRACTS | 20 M (65FT)
|||||||||||

ROLE OF STATION | NEIGHBORHOOD CENTER
|||||||||||||||||||||

SONHA STATION

DENSITY | LOW
|||||||

AREA OF PUBLIC SPACE | 0 ACRES

STATION COMPOSITION | 2 ELEMENTS
|||||||||||

SIZE OF STATION | 0.08 ACRES
|||||||||||||||||||||||||

WIDTH OF TRACTS | 22 M (73FT)
|||||||||||

ROLE OF STATION | NEIGHBORHOOD CENTER
|||||||||||||||||||||

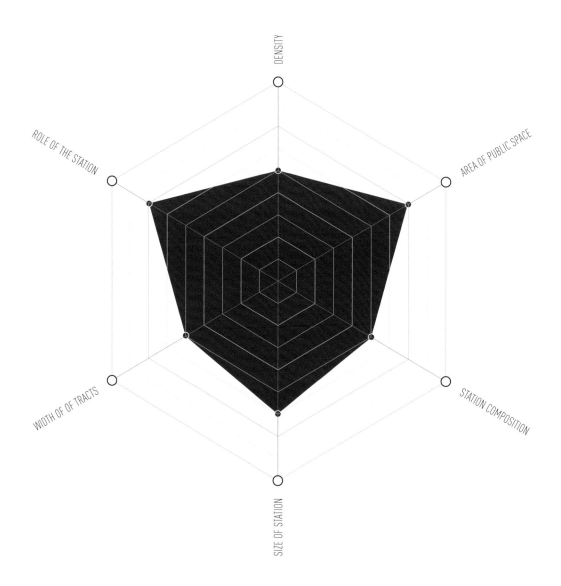

The agricultural town stations are the central stations for the smaller agrarian cities. They are the core for food production in North Korea located in the west-south side of the country. The station is surrounded by a high to medium density, but most of the parts in the city contain lower density. This type is attached to public space in front and has a medium size of the station and train tracks. However, this area will have heavy train traffic during the harvesting season. The station is composed of train tracks, station building, public space, open platform, and connection to another public transit. Agricultural town station has both side of main station and urban station typology. It is a center for the city, and at the same time, it is for the daily life of the citizens.

04 AGRICULTURAL TOWN STATION_SAMPLES

SARIWON STATION

DENSITY HIGH
||||||||||||||||||||||||||||||||||||||||

AREA OF PUBLIC SPACE 1.7 ACRES
||||||||||||||||||||||||||||||||||||||||

STATION COMPOSITION 6 ELEMENTS
||||||||||||||||||||||||||||||||||||||||

SIZE OF STATION 0.2 ACRES
||||||||||||||||||||||||||||||||||||||||

WIDTH OF TRACTS 120 M (400FT)
||||||||||||||||||||||||||||||||||||||||

ROLE OF STATION CITY CENTER
||||||||||||||||||||||||||||||||||||||||

SINMAK STATION

DENSITY HIGH
||||||||||||||||||||||||||||||||||||||||

AREA OF PUBLIC SPACE 1.7 ACRES
||||||||||||||||||||||||||||||||||||||||

STATION COMPOSITION 6 ELEMENTS
||||||||||||||||||||||||||||||||||||||||

SIZE OF STATION 0.2 ACRES
||||||||||||||||||||||||||||||||||||||||

WIDTH OF TRACTS 40 M (130FT)
||||||||||||||||||||||||||||||||||||||||

ROLE OF STATION TOWN CENTER
||||||||||||||||||||||||||||||||||||||||

PYONGSAN STATION

DENSITY MEDIUM
||||||||||||||||||||||||||||||||||||||||

AREA OF PUBLIC SPACE 1.3 ACRES
||||||||||||||||||||||||||||||||||||||||

STATION COMPOSITION 4 ELEMENTS
||||||||||||||||||||||||||||||||||||||||

SIZE OF STATION 0.2 ACRES
||||||||||||||||||||||||||||||||||||||||

WIDTH OF TRACTS 50 M (165FT)
||||||||||||||||||||||||||||||||||||||||

ROLE OF STATION TOWN CENTER
||||||||||||||||||||||||||||||||||||||||

SUKCHEON STATION

DENSITY	MEDIUM
AREA OF PUBLIC SPACE	1.6 ACRES
STATION COMPOSITION	4 ELEMENTS
SIZE OF STATION	0.2 ACRES
WIDTH OF TRACTS	40 M (130FT)
ROLE OF STATION	TOWN CENTER

TANCHON STATION

DENSITY	MEDIUM
AREA OF PUBLIC SPACE	1.4 ACRES
STATION COMPOSITION	5 ELEMENTS
SIZE OF STATION	0.3 ACRES
WIDTH OF TRACTS	92 M (300FT)
ROLE OF STATION	TOWN CENTER

JEONGJU CHEONGNYEON STATION

DENSITY	MEDIUM
AREA OF PUBLIC SPACE	2.1 ACRES
STATION COMPOSITION	5 ELEMENTS
SIZE OF STATION	0.2 ACRES
WIDTH OF TRACTS	125 M (415FT)
ROLE OF STATION	TOWN CENTER

05 INDUSTRIAL TOWN STATION _THE CHARACTERISTICS WITH THE MATRIX

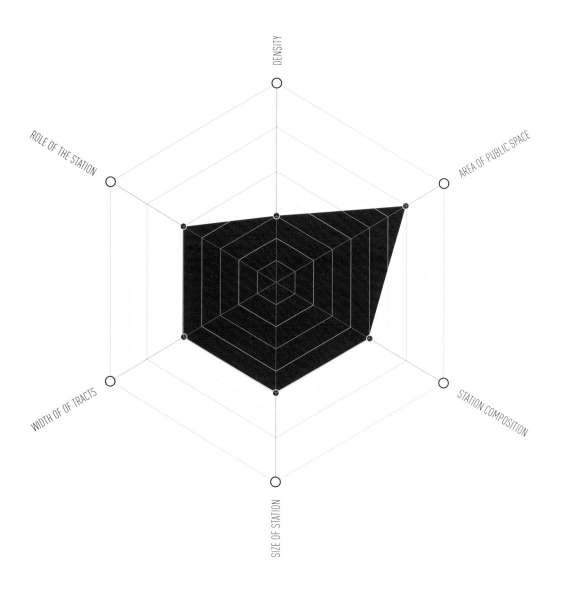

The industrial town stations are similar to the agricultural one but focused on industry, not agriculture. There is not a big difference in the composition, size, train tracks, and role of the station, it is mostly just a little smaller in dimensions. However, the surrounding is not similar. Even though there are high-density buildings around the station, the city is more spread out than an agricultural town because of all the vast factories. The industries require big spaces and broader roads. This station's tracks are of medium width because there are other transit options for distribution shipments. Therefore, this typology is a combination of industrial functions and a city center.

KUMGANG STATION

05 INDUSTRIAL TOWN STATION _SAMPLES

KIMCHEAK STATION

DENSITY	HIGH
AREA OF PUBLIC SPACE	5.1 ACRES
STATION COMPOSITION	5 ELEMENTS
SIZE OF STATION	0.2 ACRES
WIDTH OF TRACTS	100 M (325FT)
ROLE OF STATION	CITY CENTER

SONGPYEONG STATION

DENSITY	HIGH
AREA OF PUBLIC SPACE	3.8 ACRES
STATION COMPOSITION	5 ELEMENTS
SIZE OF STATION	0.3 ACRES
WIDTH OF TRACTS	115 M (375FT)
ROLE OF STATION	TOWN CENTER

SINPO STATION

DENSITY	MEDIUM
AREA OF PUBLIC SPACE	1.3 ACRES
STATION COMPOSITION	4 ELEMENTS
SIZE OF STATION	0.15 ACRES
WIDTH OF TRACTS	27 M (90FT)
ROLE OF STATION	TOWN CENTER

PANMIIN STATION

DENSITY	MEDIUM
AREA OF PUBLIC SPACE	0.7 ACRES
STATION COMPOSITION	4 ELEMENTS
SIZE OF STATION	0.4 ACRES
WIDTH OF TRACTS	50 M (165FT)
ROLE OF STATION	SPECIAL DESTINATION

MUNCHEON STATION

DENSITY	HIGH
AREA OF PUBLIC SPACE	1.2 ACRES
STATION COMPOSITION	4 ELEMENTS
SIZE OF STATION	0.15 ACRES
WIDTH OF TRACTS	38 M (125FT)
ROLE OF STATION	CITY CENTER

KWANGOK STATION

DENSITY	LOW
AREA OF PUBLIC SPACE	0 ACRES
STATION COMPOSITION	2 ELEMENTS
SIZE OF STATION	0.05 ACRES
WIDTH OF TRACTS	20 M (65FT)
ROLE OF STATION	NEIGHBORHOOD CENTER

06 VILLAGE STATION _THE CHARACTERISTICS WITH THE MATRIX

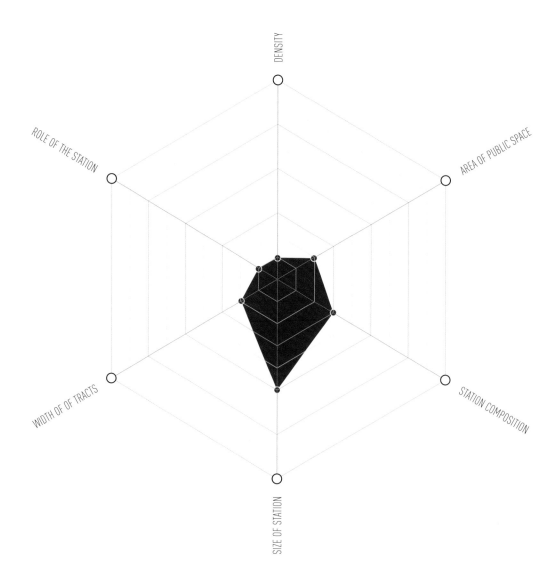

The village stations are located in rural areas, that is why the population density is the lowest. The composition of these stations is minimum, which means only train tracks, an open platform, and a station building. However, the size of the station is not the smallest in comparison because the North Korean government standardizes these structures.

There are several unique stations in this typology called special destinations. These are areas for vacationing, so even it is a small village, the users of the station would vary throughout a year.

Therefore, in this type, the building itself can be a community space for the village and sometimes for visitors.

06 VILLAGE STATION _SAMPLES

YANGDEOK STATION

DENSITY	HIGH
AREA OF PUBLIC SPACE	5.1 ACRES
STATION COMPOSITION	5 ELEMENTS
SIZE OF STATION	0.2 ACRES
WIDTH OF TRACTS	100 M (325FT)
ROLE OF STATION	CITY CENTER

CHONGGANG STATION

DENSITY	LOW
AREA OF PUBLIC SPACE	0 ACRES
STATION COMPOSITION	3 ELEMENTS
SIZE OF STATION	0.1 ACRES
WIDTH OF TRACTS	35 M (115FT)
ROLE OF STATION	NEIGHBORHOOD CENTER

CHANGRIM STATION

DENSITY	LOW
AREA OF PUBLIC SPACE	0 ACRES
STATION COMPOSITION	3 ELEMENTS
SIZE OF STATION	0.05 ACRES
WIDTH OF TRACTS	30 M (97FT)
ROLE OF STATION	NEIGHBORHOOD CENTER

YEOHYIIN STATION

DENSITY	LOW
	IIIIII
AREA OF PUBLIC SPACE	0.15 ACRES
	IIIIII
STATION COMPOSITION	3 ELEMENTS
	IIIIIIIIIIIIIIIIIII
SIZE OF STATION	0.07 ACRES
	IIIIIIIIIIIIIIIIIIII
WIDTH OF TRACTS	6 M (20FT)
	III
ROLE OF STATION	NEIGHBORHOOD CENTER
	IIIIIIIIIIIIIIIIIIIII

GWANHEA STATION

DENSITY	LOW
	IIIIII
AREA OF PUBLIC SPACE	0 ACRES
STATION COMPOSITION	3 ELEMENTS
	IIIIIIIIIIIIIIIIIII
SIZE OF STATION	0.1 ACRES
	IIIIIIIIIIIIIIIIIIIIIIIIIIIIIII
WIDTH OF TRACTS	17 M (57FT)
	IIIIII
ROLE OF STATION	TRANSPORTATION
	IIII

GEOMGANGSAN STATION

DENSITY	LOW
	IIIIII
AREA OF PUBLIC SPACE	0.9 ACRES
	IIIIIIIIIIIIIIIIIIIIIIIIIIIIIIIIIIIII
STATION COMPOSITION	5 ELEMENTS
	IIIIIIIIIIIIIIIIIIIIIIIIIIIIIII
SIZE OF STATION	0.4 ACRES
	IIIIIIIIIIIIIIIIIIIIIIIIIIIIIIII
WIDTH OF TRACTS	20 M (66FT)
	IIIIII
ROLE OF STATION	SPECIAL DESTINATION
	IIIIIIIIIIIIIIIIIIIIIIIIIIIIIIIIIIIIII

CONCLUSION _6 TYPOLOGIES AND H-LINE

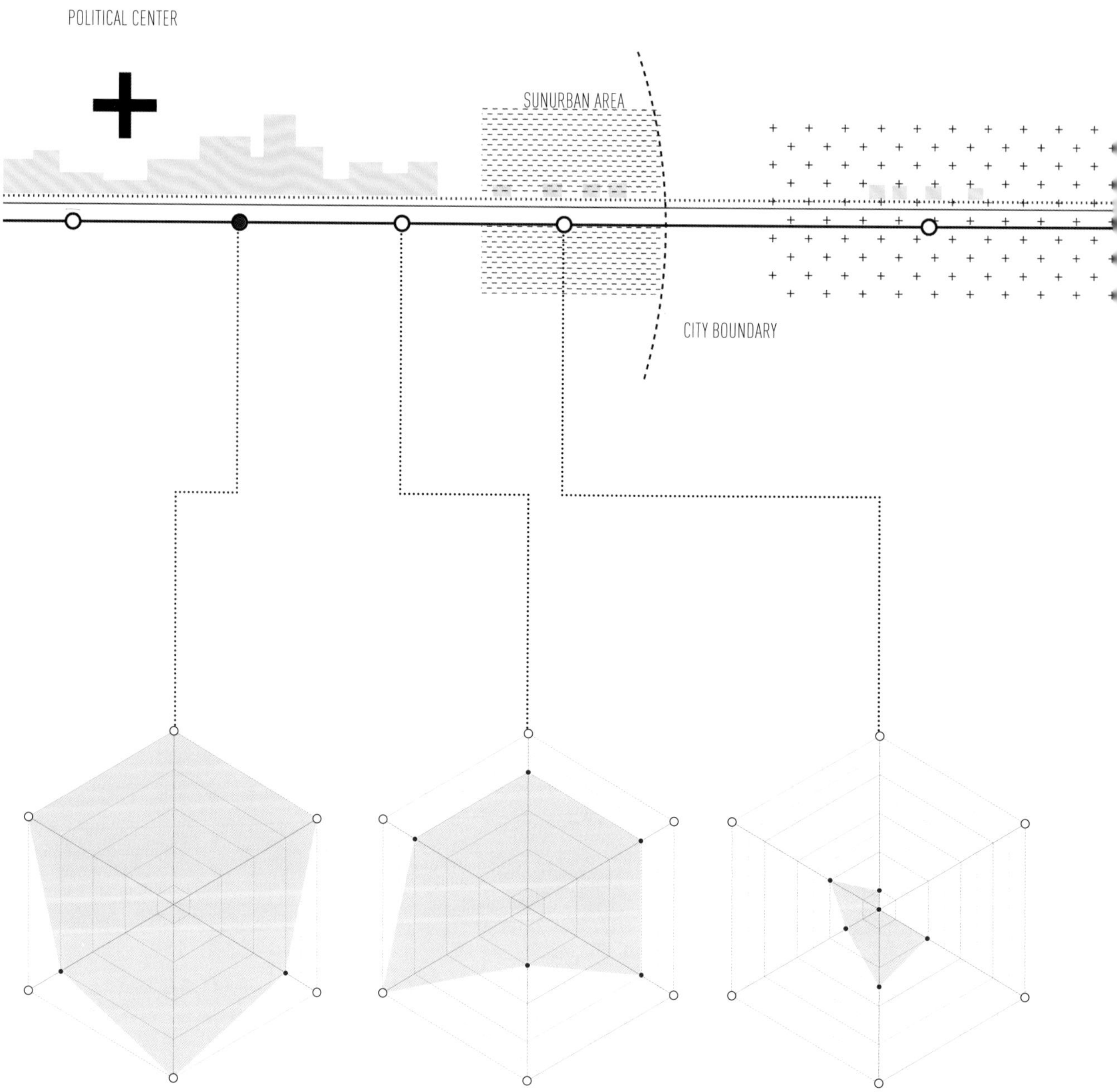

POLITICAL CENTER

SUNURBAN AREA

CITY BOUNDARY

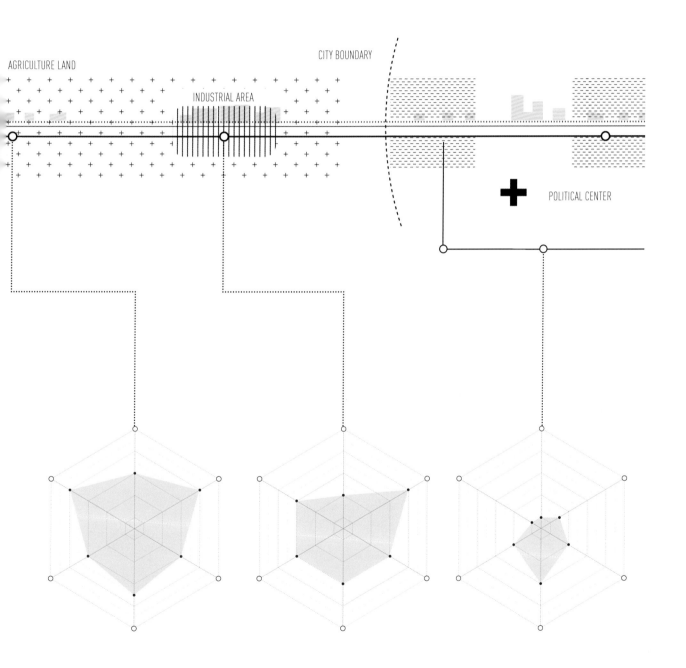

AGRICULTURE LAND

CITY BOUNDARY

INDUSTRIAL AREA

POLITICAL CENTER

H-stations
as a Catalyst

4

01

Historically, a city has a
close relationship with the
transportation network,
which North Korean cities
have lost the connection.

Stations as the Foundation of a City

Historic Relationship Between Stations and Urban Structure

Transportation is the system connecting each element of a city, the main system and in close relationship to an urban structure. As transit technologies have developed, cities have grown along the corridors. However, it was not the case for North Korea. The economy was not their spatial center but politics, which makes an awkward relationship between transit and urban structure.

It is more clear to see in the case of Pyongyang. The distribution of programs does not have any hierarchy. It is even hard to distinguish the centers.

The stations would be central areas for all the activities not only for daily life but for the economy. The primary goal is bringing back the station as a center for daily life. Moreover, the stations need to work as economic hubs by providing economic infrastructure around the stations.

STATIONS AS FOUNDATION OF A CITY_CONNECTING VARIOUS PARTS OF A CITY

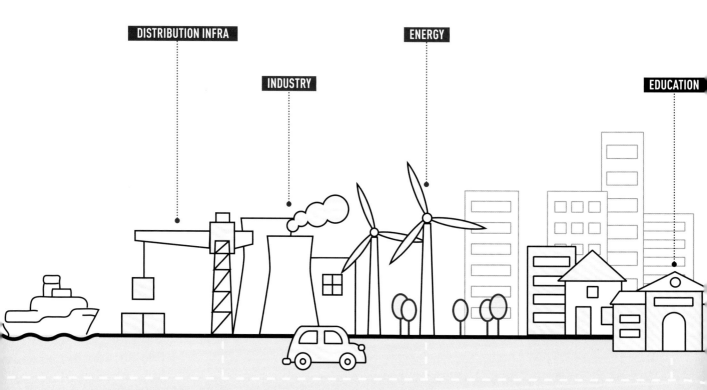

DISTRIBUTION INFRA

INDUSTRY

ENERGY

EDUCATION

TRANSIT LINE AND A CITY

Trains have been connected each part of a city and
becoming a founation in urban structure.

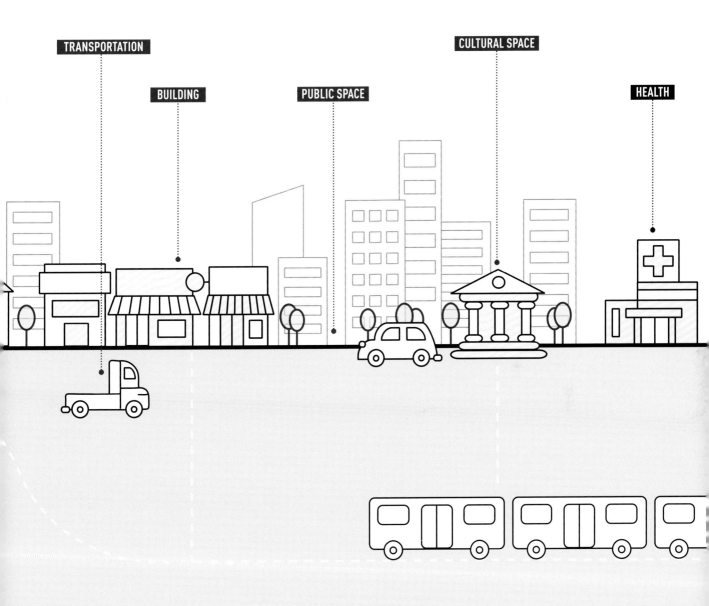

TRANSPORTATION

BUILDING

PUBLIC SPACE

CULTURAL SPACE

HEALTH

THE HISTORIC ROLE OF STATIONS_WITHIN A CITY

URBAN STRUCTURE by transportation

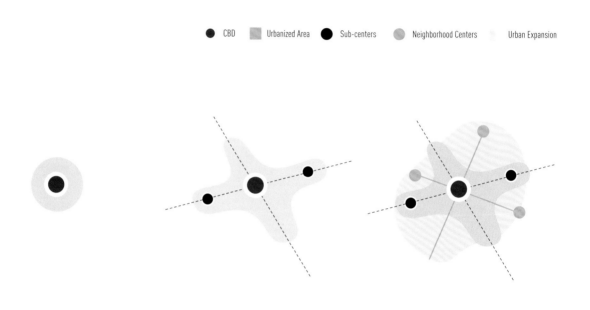

- ● CBD
- ▨ Urbanized Area
- ● Sub-centers
- ● Neighborhood Centers
- ▨ Urban Expansion

01 CARRIAGES

When a city improves their transportation system, the effects expand into their urban structure— the urban structure here meaning the distribution of density and the location of economic hubs within the city.

02 TRAINS

During the era when the carriage was the main source of transportation, the size of a city was much smaller and had only one center, due to the limitations of carriages.
After the invention of trains, cities started to grow and diversify. Sub-centers showed up along the transit

03 AUTOMOBILES

lines.
Automobiles then had a significant impact on urban structures.
Cities expanded from their prior transportation systems; still, city centers were located in transit corridors.

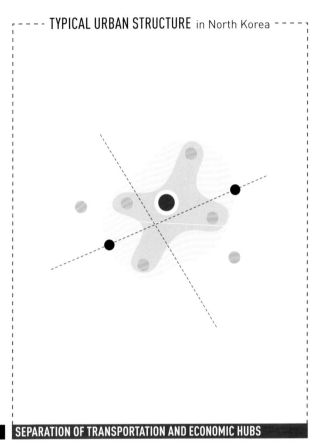

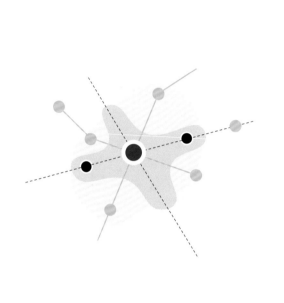

04 HIGH-SPEED TRANSPORTATION

SEPARATION OF TRANSPORTATION AND ECONOMIC HUBS

Cities become much larger with high-speed transportation because people can reach farther distances in shorter time. However, cities are still maintaining historical central areas. In the case of North Korea, it's a different story though: the country is still in the train era, moving towards automobiles their urban structure is quite exceptional considering. Because of the Korean War, their historical centers were destroyed, and their political center was rebuilt regardless of the development of their transit system. Moreover, since the government discouraged the trades in making self-sustained states, their stations have kept moving away from central areas. The separation of transportation and economic hubs makes the systems of this country more inefficient.

EXISTING URBAN STRUCTURE_IN PYONGYANG

The public programs in Pyongyang
look like they're equally distributed.
There are positive sides to this
urban structure, such as for public
services as it increases their
accessibility. However, this only
works with a good transportation
system. If their transportation
system doesn't work well, the
public services render inefficient
because these services are located
in urbanized areas, which means it's
only accessible to people already in
the city. The structures aimed for
equality, but are lacking.

Urbanized Area

Pyongyang

IIIIII Train Tracks

▬▬▬ Primary Road

───── Secondary Road

• Train Station

Green Area

River

Urbanized Area

○ Education

● Industry

● Culture

● Monument

● Office

○ Hospital

◎ Department Store

● Market

Each station typology
has a different economic
infrastructure providing
different meanings and
spaces to people.
Based on the strategies,
the new H-stations are
suggested.

H-stations as the Catalyst for Future Development

To Bring Life Back to Stations

The main goal is bringing life back to these stations; four main factors in doing this are: making the station area vibrant; land use, transportation, commercial activity, and public space.

Buildings with multiple functions are one of the core needs, but it is currently illegal in countries that have strict land-use plans like North Korea. Merely adding one more layer for land use can make it better, notably by applying the strategy only to specific areas the North Korean government wants to develop, which is an excellent way to control their developments and capitals.

Transportation is not only for people but also for products. An efficient distribution system is as essential as excellent public transportation. If H-stations are the catalyst for future development, legalized commercial activity will be the trigger. This will expand the existing markets and add lots of new markets.

The last factor in rebuilding the stations is the addition of public spaces.

These four factors have two main strategies, and each approach has several sub-elements. The combination of each element is different based on the typology of stations.

This chapter focuses on how the four approaches are applied to each typology and how the combination makes these station areas vibrant.

INTRODUCTION_THE GOAL AND STRATEGIES

01 LAND USE

- LAYERING LAND USE IN STATION ZONE

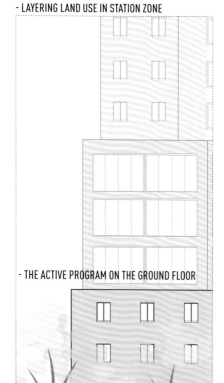

- THE ACTIVE PROGRAM ON THE GROUND FLOOR

02 TRANSPORTATION

- VARIOUS OTHER TRANSPORTATIONS

- EFFICIENT DISTRIBUTION OF PRODUCT

To achieve the goal of making North Korean stations public centers, there are eight strategies to consider. The four sectors clarified are land use, transportation, commercial activity, and public scape.

North Korea has rigorous land use, even making the ground floor of a building for retail use is illegal. Layering land use is crucial for vibrancy, therefore, by designating the station area as a particular zone, the buildings can become mixed-use, and then naturally capital will be concentrated to the station zone.

The second is the transportation of goods and people. For people, these stations are the cores of the public transportation system, but for the case of goods, using the train system as a primary resource for delivery, the backside of the station becomes a hub, sparking center efficiency.

After their strategized economic

03 COMMERCIAL ACTIVITY

- LEGALIZED MARKET AREA

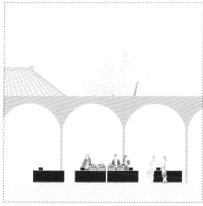

04 PUBLIC SPACE

- APPROPRIATE OUTDOOR SEATING AND GREENERY

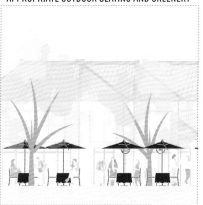

- STRIP OF RETAILS

- SCALED-DOWN PUBLIC SPACE

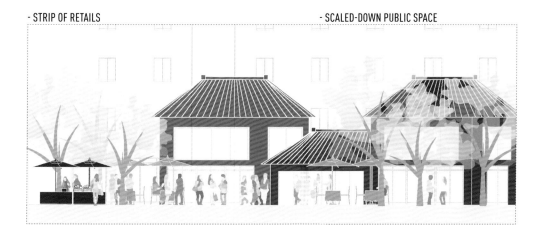

transition, this legalized commercial activity will affect urban spaces. North Koreans will participate rendering these areas as more vibrant sectors. Therefore, the structure to promote this activity is an essential strategy.

The last factor for public space and surprisingly, North Korean cities already have enough open spaces within their cities, albeit too exposed and over-scaled. North Koreans currently feel like they are being monitored in these wide-open areas, so these spaces should be refurbished with seating, activity stations, and landscape, or other essentials to fill the public spaces.

INTRODUCTION_THE ELEMENTS

01 Land use		02 Transportation	
Layering Land Use in 'Station Zone'	The Program on the Ground Floor	Various Other Transportations	Efficient Distribution of Product
COMMERCIAL	WINDOW	TRAIN / SUBWAY	TRAIN
RESIDENTIAL	DISPLAY	STREET CAR	TRAILER
AGRICULTURAL	OUTDOOR SEATING	BUS	TRUCKS
INDUSTRIAL		CAR	MORTERCYCLE
INFRASTRUCTURE		BIKE	BIKE

There are eight strategic elements to help achieve these goals, based on the typology of the train stations, the combination of factors changed, and some core necessities specific to each station (such as bike transportation).

The land-use factor is straightforward: the main programs in North Korea, except political or governmental, are commercial, residential, agricultural, industrial, and infrastructural (such as a dock or train tracks). With mixed-use programs, the ground floor is more

important than other stories for the purpose of pedestrian transactions. The windows, window displays, and especially outdoor seating are vital elements needed.

The transportation factor is based on the existing options in North Korea: from train to bike, each one

03 Commercial Activity		04 Public Space	
Legalized Market Area	Strip of Retails	Appropriate Street Furniture and Tree	Scale Downed Public Space
WHOLESALE MARKET		TREE	SMALL SCALE BUILDING
FARMERS MARKET		OUTDOOR SEATING	FOOD TRUCK
GENERAL MARKET		BENCH	STREET VENDER
RETAIL		LIGHTING	MONUMENT
		PAVED SIDEWALK	TREE

represents a hierarchy in the system. There are two types of spaces for commercial activity: one is existing markets, which are illegal currently. The other is for new retails for shaping a new commercial strip. Because these stations are the centers for transportation, these commercial elements should be aspects of the stations as well, because people will naturally gather at stations.

The main agenda for rebuilding public space is breaking down a massive open space into pieces by using various elements. First, small buildings or street vendors are divided into smaller-scale retailers. After that, the spaces should be filled with greenery and seating, establishing a more humanized space. Those elements will fill out the gap between the massive buildings, the square, and the people.

MAIN STATION_THE FOUR STRATEGIES

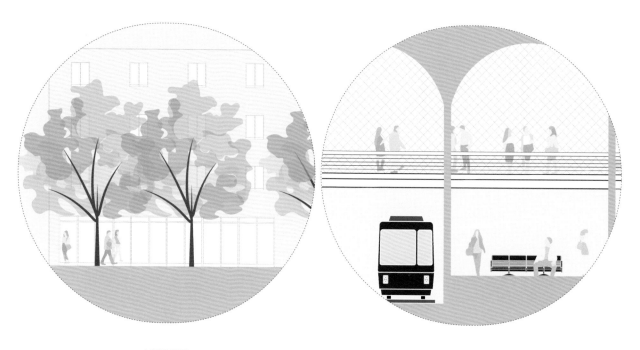

LAND USE

Attached retails and office area
Highest density in the city
Mixed-use building with retails, offices, and housings

TRANSPORTATION

Close connection to public transportation
system to each parts of the city

The main station is the most significant type of station. It is surrounded by the highest-density population and is the largest in size. After their economic transition, this area should be the busiest in North Korea.

After the area surrounding the main station is designated as a "station zone," the ground floor within the building will become a space for restaurants and retails, attracting tourists and pedestrians using the station. Furthermore, because of the convenience of transit, more

businesses will settle around these main stations. The main station would have more functions than just simply used for transportation. It would be a multi-functional space. The main station would a center for the transportation of people rather than goods. There would be more

COMMERCIAL ACTIVITY

Symbolic facade showing the identity of the city
Attached retails and office area
Place for tourists

PUBLIC SPACE

Symbolic facade showing the identity of the city
Place for tourists

purpose for pedestrian traffic than for industrial or distribution purposes. As the main hub station for all public transportation, people would be able take a subway, streetcar, or bus after exiting the train.

The vast square would, at this point, been rebuilt as an active public space with various commercial uses. There would be shopping areas as well as restaurants or cafes. Street vendors would start to fill up space, and the addition of greenery would add to the aesthetic and comfort of the space.

The station itself would be a tourist spot. The uniqueness of design would further attract pedestrian traffic who would be able to see the cityscape from the station.

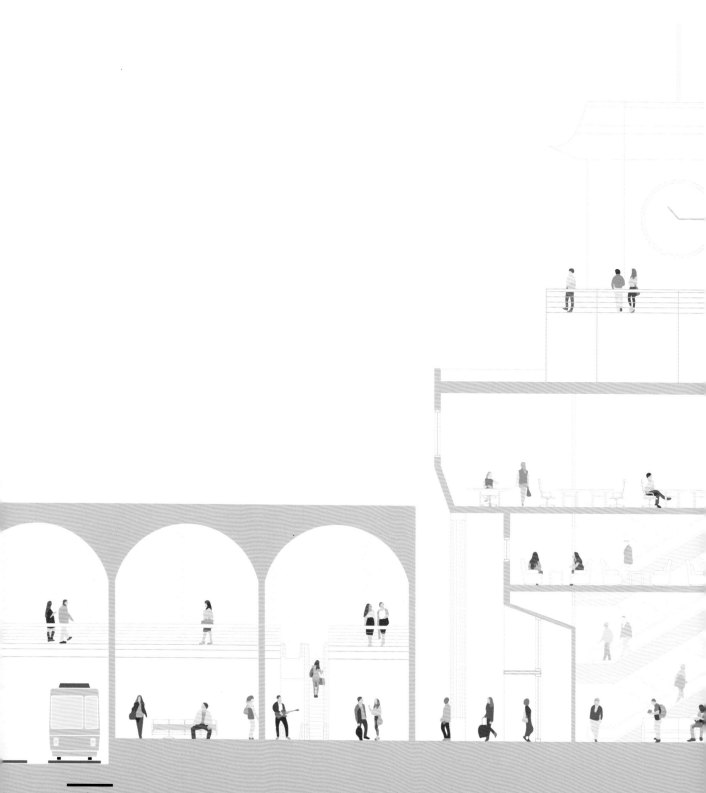

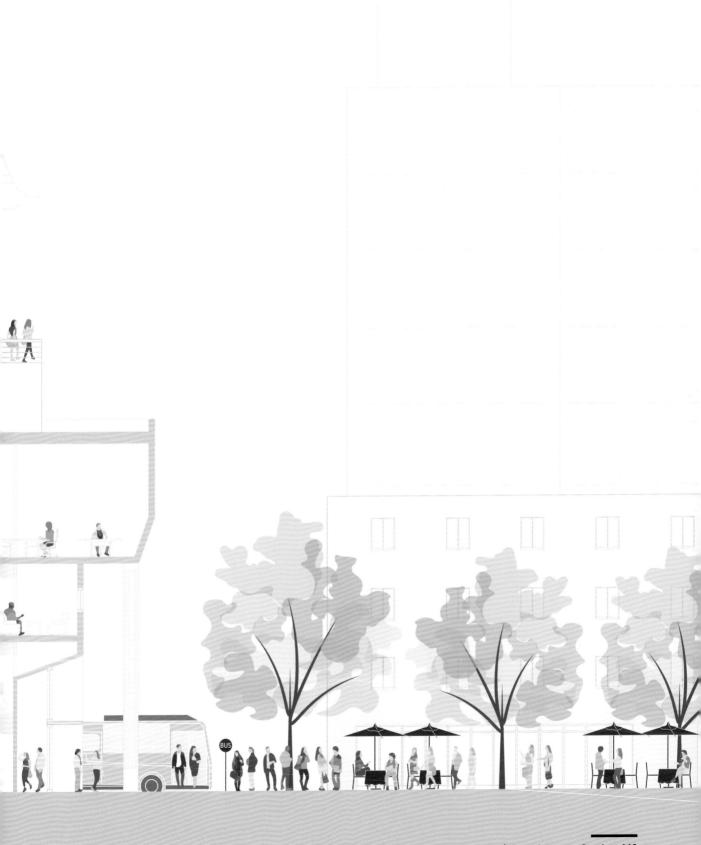

URBAN STATION_THE FOUR STRATEGIES

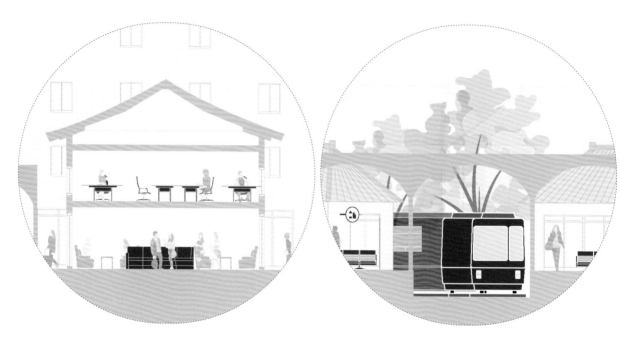

LAND USE

2-3 stories station with Retails attached
Medium Density Mixed-use Buildings
Renovated the First Floor to Office or Housing

TRANSPORTATION

Central station for distribution of goods and
industries in the city
Close connection to public transportation
to Each Neighborhoods

The urban station type is within a sub-center of a city before or following the main station or central station of smaller towns. Therefore, the size of this station type is smaller than the main station, but the surrounding population is still pretty high. This station is more for the residents than visitors.

This area would have mixed-use buildings but not as radical as the main station. The change would be smaller and slower due to the station's nature and size, so it should have simple, functional spaces.

In the case of transportation, unlike the main stations, it would be the central hub for industrial and distribution purposes. It would have fuller train tracks than the main station since it would be dealing with additional functions that the main station would not be able to handle due to higher pedestrian

COMMERCIAL ACTIVITY

Commercials focused on daily life
Places for after work and weekends

PUBLIC SPACE

The center for daily life

traffic. Of course, it would have close connections to other public transportations, connecting each neighborhood.

Existing markets are usually located around urban stations, so these existing markets would grow and affect much of the surrounding, however, these markets would be for daily necessities, not luxury products. Therefore, the scale of each retailer would be small and focused on something people can do after work or during weekends.

Naturally, the public space alongside urban stations would be similar to commercial areas. Along with the markets, there would be greenery and public seating next to pedestrian roads, making the space more dynamic and lively.

SUBURBAN STATION_THE FOUR STRATEGIES

TRANSPORTATION

Smaller Scale of Public Transportation
Distribution of food production

The suburban station type is the byproduct of socialist planning, to prevent the growth of a city. These stations are located within the jurisdiction of a big city, however, the density and characteristics are similar to the rural area station types. This area is for food production in its town.

The surrounding area does not have a high enough density to need mixed-use and because of that, this area quickly becomes a target for developers, incurring suburbanization. Therefore, it is essential to control the developments by these stations.

The primary user of these

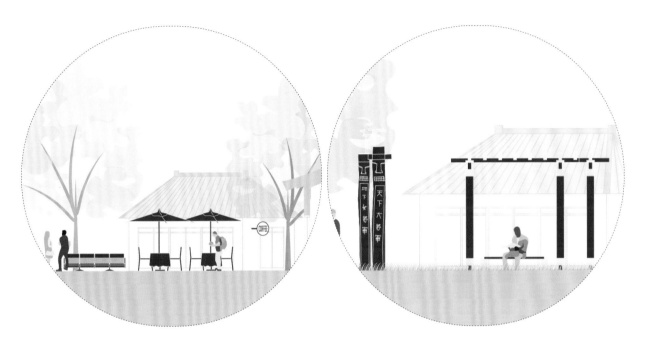

COMMERCIAL ACTIVITY

Several small retails around the station

PUBLIC SPACE

Small scale public space for the residents

stations is the residents and the food products. There would be spaces and infrastructure for food distribution mainly using trains and some vehicles. Due to the smaller population, public transportation is on a smaller scale with fewer options.

The commercial activities are of two extremes: one is small trade within the village, and the other is with all other cities, which need the product of the town. The small retailers and offices are located around the station. With the small center, there would be a smaller-scale public space for residents where they can take rest and gather.

AGRICULTURAL TOWN STATION_THE FOUR STRATEGIES

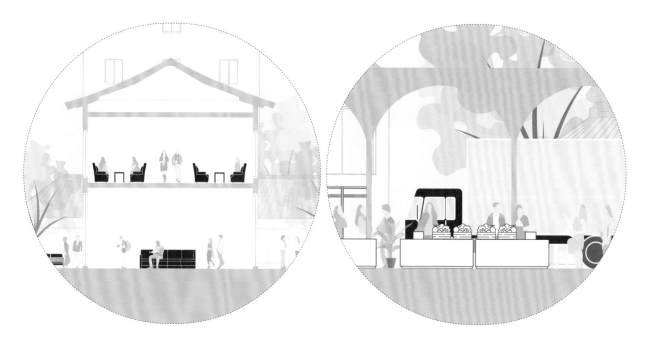

LAND USE

Mideum density mixed-use surrounding
buildingd and the station

TRANSPORTATION

Distribution system for food production in
wholesale, retail, and personal scale

The agricultural town station type is located in the middle of productive land. Most agricultural industries are concentrated in these areas and the stations would be hubs for the trade and distribution. The surroundings would have medium density in population and the station would be the central station for these towns. The food industry is the main focus for these towns, so, these station zones would include a combination of retailers for the community and places for food markets. With the station, the market area is the catalyst, making it vibrant. There are spaces designated within the distribution system for each

COMMERCIAL ACTIVITY

Commercial activities in various scale from
wholesale to smaller scale such as farmers market

PUBLIC SPACE

Market space as a public and social space

commercial scale. For instance, some of the products would go directly to the train, others would go to trailers or trucks for individual retailers. That means the products come from the outskirts of towns to the stations and then to each part of the country.

This active commercial activity affects local business as they coexist and can positively effect each other. In the case of public space, the market has historically been an important social space in Korea. The market is a public space itself and this function affects the surrounding and broadens it.

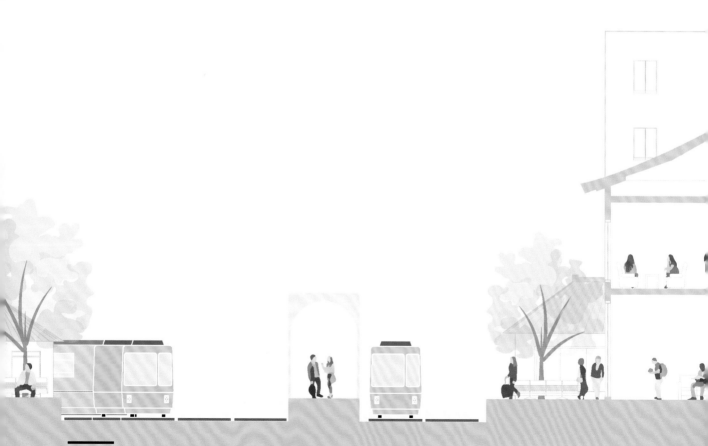

INDUSTRIAL TOWN STATION_THE FOUR STRATEGIES

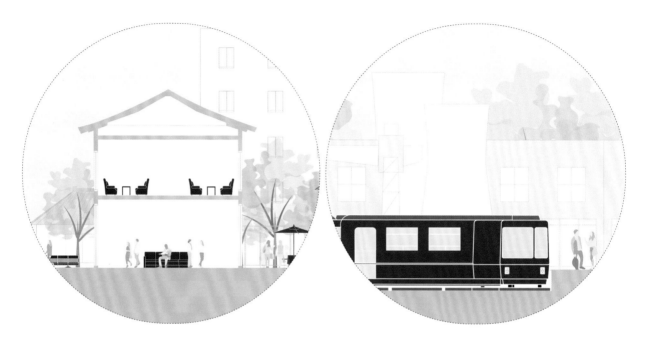

LAND USE

Higher density mixed-use around station but
lower density in the outskirt of the town

TRANSPORTATION

Heavy industrial use and the public
transportation in a smaller scale

The industrial town station type has similar characteristics to the agricultural town station, except the distribution of density and program. In this town, there is a higher density in the station and factories, but not the market area.

The transportation in this town is for delivering the source materials for the industries and then the final product to other cities or other countries. These sectors are various throughout the country based on the assets that are has. For instance, the industries on the left side of

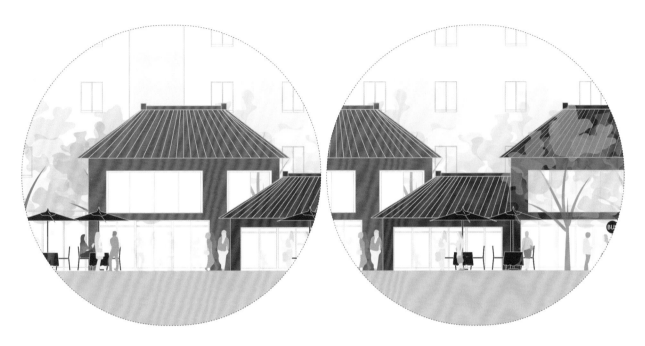

COMMERCIAL ACTIVITY

Mainly for the residents and partially for
business and tourists

PUBLIC SPACE

Spaces for daily life and scale-downed with
smaller buildings or street vendors

H-line focus on heavy industries with sufficient energy sources. The most common use of public transportation would be the bus or streetcar in these industrial towns. This is because the economy here is not active enough to support the subway. The commercial activity and public spaces are similar to that of the urban station type. They are mostly for residents and there are few places for business and tourists. The open space in front of the station is scaled down with smaller buildings, street vendors, and greenery.

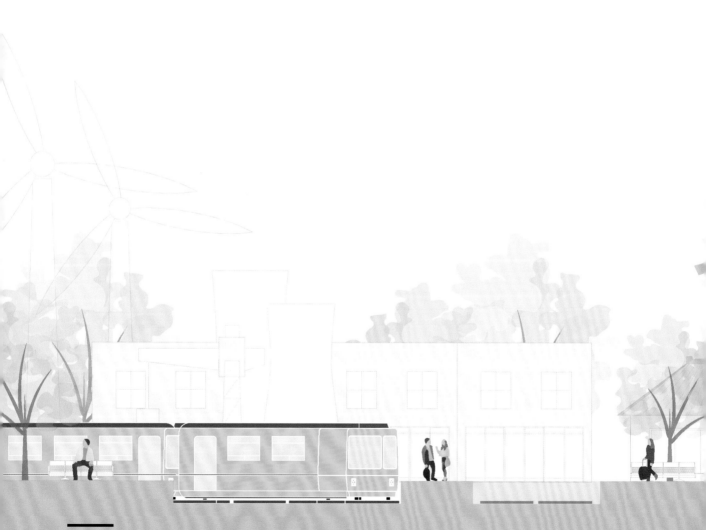

TRANSPORTATION

Personal car, motorcycle, or bike is the most
common

The village station type is located in rural areas. Almost 50 percent of H-stations are under this category type. The densities here are the lowest, which means there is no need for mixed-use buildings.

However, still, the station zone is the center of the village. The difference is the station is the community center here, not the surroundings. Therefore, commercial activities are concentrated here.

In the case of public space, due to the density, there is vast outdoor space. But putting a pavilion or exercise facility, this area can be well used.

COMMERCIAL ACTIVITY

The station itself becomes community center
which has little retails inside

PUBLIC SPACE

Small pavilion close to the station as a outdoor
gathering space in this town

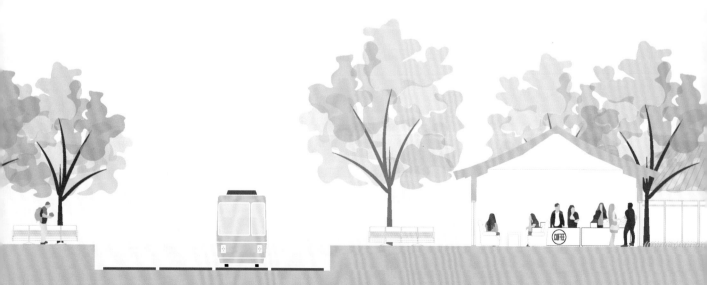

CONCLUSION_THE STATIONS

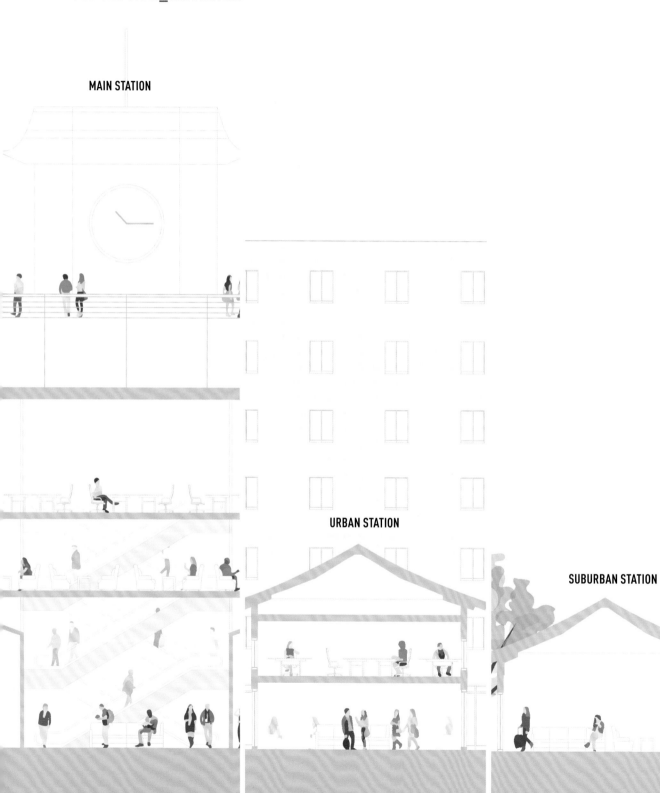

MAIN STATION

URBAN STATION

SUBURBAN STATION

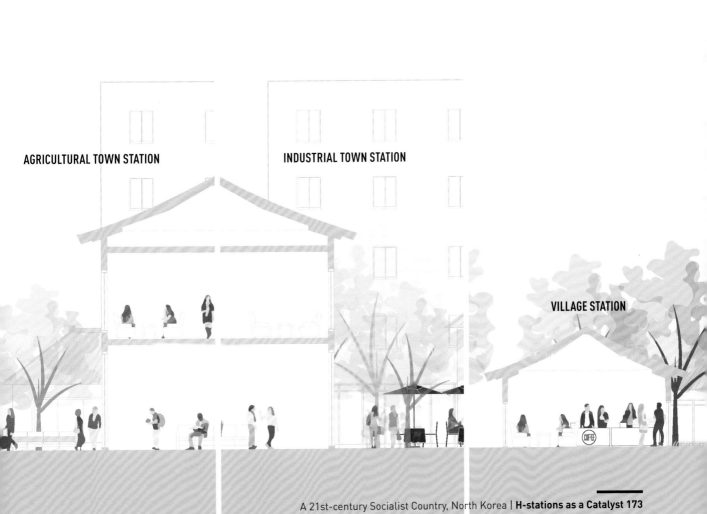

AGRICULTURAL TOWN STATION

INDUSTRIAL TOWN STATION

VILLAGE STATION

Outro

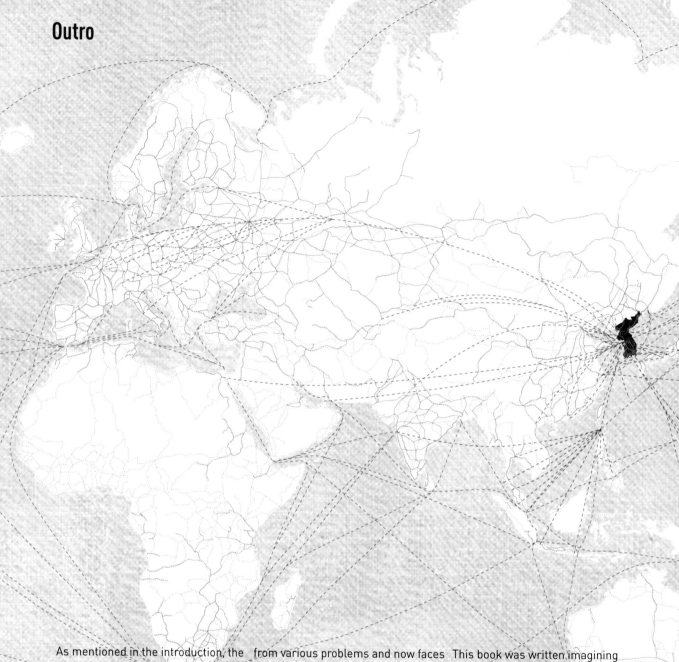

As mentioned in the introduction, the two primary purposes of the book are to focus on the potential North Korea has for development and arguing the necessity for further research. No one knows what North Korea's future development will look like, however, this country has suffered from various problems and now faces an inevitable moment of change. Moreover, if this change occurs, it will affect the surrounding countries, especially South Korea. To control these effects we need to keep an eye on North Korea.

This book was written imagining the future of North Korea as a sustainable country but at the same time looking at the pressing issues that the country has. Hopefully, through this book, people can experience both sides, reality and vision.

REFERENCES_

Book

Dempsey, N. *Future Forms and Design for Sustainable Cities*. Amsterdam: Elsevier. 2005.

Kim, W. 사회주의 도시계획 [*Socialist City Planning*]. Bosunggak. 1998.

Kwon, Y., et al. *Understanding Urban Planning in the City of Pyongyang*. Korea: The Seoul Institute. 1998.

Lee, J., et al. *The National Atlas of Korea I*. Korea: National Geographic Information Institute. 2014.

Lee, J., et al. *The National Atlas of Korea II*. Korea: National Geographic Information Institute. 2014.

Lee, J., et al. *The National Atlas of Korea III*. Korea: National Geographic Information Institute. 2014.

Lee, S., et al. *North Korean Land and Housing Review*. Korea: Land and Housing Institute. 2017.

Pedret, A. *Pyongyang 2050: Spatial Futures*. Damdi. 2018.

Yim, D. *Un Precedented Pyongyang*. Actar. 2016.

Yim, D. and Luna, R. *North Korean Atlas*. Damdi. 2014.

Journal

Beak, J. and Yoon, J. "6.25 전쟁에 대한 연구: 결과와 영향을 중심으로" ["Study About 6.25 War: Focus on the Result and Influence"]. 국사관논총, no. 28 (1991).

Cho, N. "북한의 도시화 추이와 특징" ["The Trend and Characteristics of Urbanization in North Korea"]. *KDI Review of the North Korean Economy*, no. 05 (2013): pp.39-60.

Han, S. "Spatial Transformation of the Cities in East Germany and Eastern Europe in Post-socialist Era: Implications for Unified Korea." *Journal of the Korean Urban Management Association*, no. 24 (2011): pp.125-141.

Heo, S. "1945년 해방과 대한민국 경제 발전" ["Korea's Liberation in 1945 and its Economic Development"]. 한국독립운동사연구, no. 04 (2012): pp.463-509.

Jo, S. "북한의 도시개발-평양시를 중심으로" ["The Urban Development of North Korea-Focus on Pyongyang]. 국사편찬회, no. 70 (1996): pp.142-207.

Jung, U. "북한 시장의 발전과정에 대한 연구" ["A Study on the Development Process of the North Korean Market"]. 수은북한경제 (2014): pp.47-76.

Kim, C. "독일통일 25년, 구동독지역 인구 및 노동력 변화" ["Twenty-Five Years of German Unification, Population, and Labor Change in the Driving Directions"]. *KDI Review of the North Korean Economy*, no. 03 (2015): pp.29-45.

Kim, D. "Railroad of North Korea, 1900-2015: Implications on Its Industrialization and Economic Decline." 경제사학회, no. 65, (2017): pp.335-369.

Kim, H. "Overview of the Nutritional Status and Policy Directions of Supporting Children's Nutrition in North Korea." 보건복지포럼, Unknown (2007): pp.24-34.

Kim, K. "북한의 물자원" ["Water Resource of North Korea"]. *Korean National Committee on Irrigation and Drainage Transaction*, no. 09 (2013): pp.63-71.

Kim, M. "동유럽 주요국의 경제체제 전환과정-폴란드, 체코슬로바키아, 헝가리를 중심으로" ["The Transformation of Economic System in Major Countries of Eastern Europe - Focused on Poland, Czechoslovakia and Hungary"]. 산은경제연구소, no. 615 (2007): pp.1-39.

Kim, M. and Jung, I. "The Transformation of Pyongyang's Urban Morphology after the Late Joseon Period - Through the Comparison of Pyongyangseongdo and Land Register Map of 1914." *Journal of the Architectural Institute of Korea Planning & Design*, no. 29 (2013): pp.217-226.

Kim, M., Lee, T., and Ban, Y. "Analysis of Urban Spatial Configuration between Seoul and Pyongyang City Using Space Syntax." 한국도시행정학회 도시행정학보, no. 25 (2012): pp.161-179.

Kim, R., et al. "Estimation of Land Cover and Vegetation Change in North Korea Using Satellite Data." 국토연구, no. 90 (2016): pp.117-128.

Kim, S. "2015년 상반기 북한 시장과 사경제 동향" ["North Korean Market and Private Economy Trends in the First Half of 2015"]. *KDI Review of the North Korean Economy*, no. 8 (2015): pp.52-61.

Kim, T. "Overturned Time and Space: Drastic Changes in the Daily Lives of North Koreans During the Korean War." *Asian Journal of Peacebuilding*, no. 2 (2014): pp.241-262.

Kim, Y. "2017년 북한 농업 주요 동향과 전망" ["Major Trends and Prospects of North Korean Agriculture in 2017"]. *KDI Review of the North Korean Economy*, no. 2 (2018): pp.71-80.

Kim, Y., et al. "After the Liberation, The Comparative Study on the Spatial Construction and the Characteristics of the Urban Central Place in Seoul and Pyongyang - Centered on Spatial, Political, and Economic Perspectives." *Journal of the Architectural Institute of Korea Planning & Design*, no. 17 (2001): pp.31-42.

Kotz, D. M. "Lessons from Economic Transition in Russia and China." *Political Economy and Contemporary Capitalism: Radical Perspectives on Economic Theory and Policy*, (2000): pp.210-217.

Lee, J. "선택받은 도시, 평양과 평양사람들" ["Selected City, Pyongyang and the People"]. *Critical Review of History*, no. 11 (2013): pp.96-115.

Lee, S. "The Possibility of Pyeongyang, the City of 'Socialism with a Korean Heart, Becoming an East Asian City.'" *The Journal of Korean History*, no. 137 (2007): pp.143-179.

Lee, S. "북한의 주거환경 개선을 위한 남북협력 실천과제" ["South-North Cooperation for the Improvement of Housing Environment in North Korea"]. *KDI Review of the North Korean Economy*, no. 7 (2015): pp.31-41p.

Lee, S. "2017년 북한의 산업동향" ["North Korea's Industrial Trend in 2017"]. *KDI Review of the North Korean Economy*, no. 2 (2018): pp.31-39.

Lim, C. "북한의 산업현황과 남북한 경제의 보완성 분석" ["A Study on the Industrial Status of North Korea and the Economic Complementation of South and North Korea"]. 금융경제연구, no. 178 (2004).

Myeong, S. "북한의 환경 현황" ["Current Situation of Environment in North Korea"]. *KDI Review of the North Korean Economy*, no. 3 (2018): pp.41-59.

Park, J. "The Process of Opening of Inland Market and the Nature of Mixed Residence in Pyeongyang of the Open Port Period." *Han'guk Munhwa: Korean Culture*, no. 64 (2013): pp.77-118.

Shin, G., and Jung, I. "Appropriating the Socialist Way of Life: The Emergence of Mass Housing in post-war North Korea." *The Journal of Architecture*, no. 21 (2016): pp.159-180.

https://doi.org/10.1080/13602365.2016.1156143
Summary National Policy Strategy for Infrastructure and Spatial Planning. (n.d.). 24.

Tak, H., Kim, S., and Son, I. "A Study on Distributions and Spatial Properties of Geomorphological Mountain Area." 대한지리학회지, no. 48 (2013): pp.1-18.

Thesis

Dornbusch, R., Wolf, H., and Alexander, L. "Economic Transition in Eastern Germany." *Brookings Papers on Economic Activity*, 1992(1), 235. 1992. https://doi.org/10.2307/2534560.

Kim, K. (2016). "An Empirical Analysis on the Infrastructure Investment Facilitation toward North Korea: Lessons from Transition Countries." Master's thesis, Hanyang University, 2016.

Kim, M. "A Study on the Planning of Microdistricts in Post-War North Korea." PhD diss., Hanyang University, 2018.

Kim, S. "A Study on the Changes of Spatial Structure of Pyeongyang and Tasks after Reunification." Master's thesis, University of Seoul, 2016.

Kwak, E. "The Analysis of Space Symbolism in North Korea Focusing on Kim Jong Il and Kim Jong Un's On-The-Spot-Guidance during Their Initial Four Years of Reign." Master's thesis, Korea University, 2016.

Qian, Y., and Jinglian, W. "China's Transition to a Market Economy: How Far Across the River? In S. Ichimura, T. Sato, & W. James (Eds.)." *Transition from Socialist to Market Economies*, pp.37-66. Palgrave Macmillan UK: 2000. https://doi.org/10.1057/9780230244986_3.

Report

Anonymous. *Randstad 2040 Summary of the Structural Vision* (Report No. Unknown). Ministry of Housing, Spatial Planning and the Environment, 2008.

Anonymous. *Summary National Policy Strategy for Infrastructure and Spatial Planning*. The Hague: Ministry of Infrastructure and the Environment, 2011.

Anonymous. *Icons of Dutch Spatial Planning* (Report No. Unknown). Den Haag: Ministry of Infrastructure and the Environment, 2012.

Anonymous. 2016 북한 이해 [*2016 Understanding North Korea*] (Report No. Unknown). Korea: Unification Education, 2016.

Anonymous. *2017 Annual Report on Wind Energy Industry in Korea* (Report No. Unknown). Korea: Korea Wind Energy Industry Association, 2018.

Anonymous. 2019 북한 이해 [*2019 Understanding North Korea*] (Report No. Unknown). Korea: Unification Education, 2019.

Ha, N. 체제전환국의 정부 간 재정관계 변화 분석 [*Analysis of Governmental Financial Relationship in Transition Countries*](Report No. Unknown). Korea: Korean Institute of Local Finance, 2018.

Hong, M., et al. 북한 전국 시장 정보: 공식시장 현황을 중심으로 [*North Korea's National Market Information: Focusing on the Status of Official Markets*] (Report No. 16-24). Korea: Korea Institute for National Unification, 2017.

Hwang, S. *Major Statistics Indicators of North Korea* (Report No. 2005-5242). Korea: Statistics Korea, 2017.

Im, G. 북한경제의 비공식(시장)부문 실태분석: 기업활동을 중심으로 [*An Analysis of the Informal (market) Sector of North Korea's Economy: Business Activities*] (Report No. 13-11). Korea: Korea Institute for National Unification, 2013.

Jeon, H. 2007년도 농업과학기술개발사업 주요연구성과 [*The Results of the 2007 Agricultural Science and Technology Development Project*] (Report No. Unknown). Korea: Rural Development Administration, 2008.

Jeon, S. 북한, 도시로 읽다 [*North Korea, As a City*] (Report No. Unknown). Korea: Korea Institute for National Unification, 2015.

Jeong, H., et al. *Determinants of Economic Growth in Transition Economies: Their Implications for North Korea* (Report No. 14-01). Korea: Korea Institute for International Economic Policy, 2014.

Jeong, J. 중국의 주요 경제사회지표 [*The Economic-Social Statistics in China*] (Report No.101-161). Korea: Statistics Korea, 1996.

Jeong, J. 통독전후의 경제사회상 비교 [*Comparison of Economic-Social Statistics Before and After Unification in Germany*] (Report No.101-59). Korea: Statistics Korea, 1996.

Kim, S., et al. 북한의 경제전환 모형: 사회주의국가의 경험이 주는 함의 [*North Korea's Model for Economic Transformation: The Meaning of the Experience of the Socialist State*] (Report No. 2001-06). Korea: Korea Institute for National Unification, 2001.

Kin, H. 서울과 평양의 도시계획 이념 및 공간구조 비교 [*Comparison of Urban Planning Ideology and Spatial Structure between Seoul and Pyongyang*] (Report No. 2004-PR-12). Korea: Seoul Development Institute, 2004.

Lee, S., et al. *A Projection of Migration Flows after South-North Korea Integration and Policy Measures* (Report No. 2012-47-13). Korea: 한국보건사회연구원, 2012.

Lee, S., Yang, M., and Jung, U. 북한 시장실태 분석 [*Analysis of North Korean Market Situation*] (Report No. 2014-738). Korea: Korea Institute for Industrial Economics & Trade, 2014.

Moon, I., et al. 중국 국유기업의 개혁에 대한 평가 및 시사점 [*Evaluation and Implications of Reform in China's State-Owned Enterprises*] (Report No. Unknown). Korea: Korea Institute for International Economic Policy, 2014.

Sagong, H., Seo, G., and Han, S. *Methods to Survey on the Status of Use of Territory in North Korea* (Report No. 2006-38). Korea: Korea Research Institute for Human Settlements, 2006.

Seo, S. 북한의 산업입지 현황 및 적정 산업배치 모형 [*Current Status of Industrial Location in North Korea and Optimal Industrial Layout Model*] (Report No. PAMP1000012534). Korea: Korea Institute for International Economic Policy, 2004.

United Nation. *2019 DPR Korea Needs and Priorities* (Report No. Unknown). Unknown: United Nation, 2019.

Yoon, D., Jung, H., and Nam, Y. *Possible Scenario for Financial Reform in North Korea Based on the Experiences of Transition Countries* (Report No. 02-18). Korea: Korea Institute for International Economic Policy, 2002.

Yoon, S., et al. 재생가능에너지 대북 지원 제도 및 협력 방안 연구 [*A Study on the Renewable Energy Support System and Cooperation for North Korea*] (Report No. Unknown). Korea: 서울대학교 통일평화연구원, 2008.

Etc.

Blog of Gyeonggi Research Institute. Accessed 2017. https://m.blog.naver.com/PostView. nhn?blogId=gri_blog&logNo=220957547606&proxyReferer=https%3A%2F%2Fwww.google. com%2F

Chung, W. 에너지수급브리프 [*Energy Supply Brief*], Korea: Korea Energy Economics Institute, 2018.

Lee, G. 북한의 수자원과 공유하천 관리 [*Water Resources and Stream Management in North Korea*]. Korea: K-Water, 2015.

Senate Department for Urban Development. *Berlin Strategy: Urban Development Concept Berlin 2030*. Berlin: Senate Department for Urban Development, 2015.

IMAGE CREDITS_

Anonymous. Tongil Geori Market.
http://naenara.com.kp/ko/

Jangmadang
Anonymous. 2019 북한 이해 [*2019 Understanding North Korea*] (Report No. Unknown).
Korea: Unification Education, (2019).

Anonymous. "Arturo Soria y Mata." 1844. *Royal Academy of History.*
http://dbe.rah.es/biografias/8378/arturo-soria-y-mata.

Anonymous. "Ebenezer Howard." 1964. *Welwyn Garden City Library.*
https://www.ourwelwyngardencity.org.uk/content/people/ebenezer_howard.

Anonymous. "Portrait of Karl Marx." *International Institute of Social History*
(Amsterdam).
https://iisg.amsterdam/en/detail?id=https%3A%2F%2Fiisg.amster-
dam%2Fid%2Fitem%2F696310.

Anonymous. "Portrait of Friedrich Engels." 1879. *International Institute of Social
History.* http://www.unesco.org/new/fileadmin/MULTIMEDIA/HQ/CI/images/mow/
netherlands_germany_engels.jpg.

Anonymous. "Vladimir Lenin." *Encyclopedia Britannica.*
https://www.britannica.com/biography/Vladimir-Lenin#/media/1/335881/137007.

Day, Michael. "Keasung Apartment Block." 2011. *Flickr.*
https://www.flickr.com/photos/whoisthatfreakwiththecamera/6647245693/.

Gilliland, Clay. "Department Store Wonsan DPRK." 2014. *Flickr.* https://www.flickr.
com/photos/26781577@N07/14885617026/in/photolist-2yLhRf-2yFUqg-P2FLKn-
pn4HtG-4Y7gcE-2yFSNe-9ox9ni-4Y31sv-9jSecE-afMmsK-gQjGNW-25uMaQt-EhCVXK-
29U79uz-oFoFkq-4acooC-UGx7T5-rtgRYr.

Harak, Roman. "North Korea, Keasung." 2010. *Flickr.*
https://www.flickr.com/photos/roman-harak/5015883510/.

Harak, Roman. "North Korea, Kim Il-Sung Statue." 2010. *Flickr.*
https://www.flickr.com/photos/roman-harak/5015232313/.

Krasowski, Stefan. "North Korea 056." 2010. *Flickr.*
https://www.flickr.com/photos/rapidtravelchai/6160331579/.

Morgan, Jen. "Pyongyang." 2012. *Flickr.* https://www.flickr.com/photos/momoci-
ta/6822853476/in/album-72157629555978377/.

Morgan, Jen. "Pyongyang." 2012. *Flickr.*
https://www.flickr.com/photos/momocita/6822805138/.

Morgan, Jen. "North Korean Countryside." 2012. *Flickr.*
https://www.flickr.com/photos/momocita/6822844214/in/al-
bum-72157629555978377/.

Nicholson, Caitriana. "North Korea." 2012. *Flickr.*
https://www.flickr.com/photos/caitriana/7730894462/.

Org, Alpari. "North Korea Currency - North Korean Won." 2019. *Flickr.*
https://www.flickr.com/photos/162793571@N04/48085888817/.

Sloan, Dan. "Pyongyang." 2011. *Flickr.* https://www.flickr.com/photos/dantoujo-
urs/15213768896/.

Stanley, David. "Ministry Building, Pyongyang." 2010. *Flickr.*
https://www.flickr.com/photos/davidstanleytravel/5063726602/.

Stephan. "North Korea, Keasung." 2007. *Flickr.*
https://www.flickr.com/photos/fljckr/1027504260/.

Tours, Uri. "Hamhung." 2014. *Flickr.*
https://www.flickr.com/photos/northkoreatravel/14297976844/.

Tours, Uri. "Unha Scientist Street." 2013. *Flickr.*
https://www.flickr.com/photos/northkoreatravel/16047482955/in/al-
bum-72157649751283236/.

Warby, William. "North Korea." 2018. *Flickr.* https://www.flickr.com/photos/wwar-
by/46173737274/.